DOUGLAS STUART MOORE

Douglas Moore was born in Cutchogue, New York, in 1893. He studied at Yale with Horatio Parker and D. S. Smith and then, after a tour in the navy, he studied with d'Indy at the Schola Cantorum in Paris, and with Nadia Boulanger. He was later a student of Ernest Bloch in Cleveland. In 1924 he won the Pulitzer Traveling Scholarship, and in 1933 received a Guggenheim Fellowship.

In 1940 Moore succeeded Daniel Gregory Mason as head of Columbia's music department and was appointed MacDowell Professor of Music in 1945. From 1946 to 1952 he was president of the National Institute of Arts and Letters; he was president of the American Academy from 1960 to 1962 and is currently a member of its board of directors. He has received the degree of Doctor of Music from the Cincinnati Conservatory and Syracuse and Yale universities. He has appeared as guest conductor with several leading American orchestras. His Symphony in A major received Honorable Mention by the New York Critics Circle in 1947.

His works have had numerous performances all over the world. *The Devil and Daniel Webster,* his earliest opera, was first performed on May 18, 1939, with Fritz Reiner conducting. *Giants in the Earth* won him the Pulitzer Prize in Music in 1951. He won the New York Critics Circle Award in Opera in 1958, for *The Ballad of Baby Doe,* which was commissioned by the Koussevitzky Foundation and was first performed in Central City, Colorado, July 7, 1956. Five years later it was performed in Europe. His most recent opera, *Wings of the Dove,* had its first performance at the New York City Center in 1961.

Besides the present volume, Douglas Moore is the author of *A Guide to Musical Styles: From Madrigal to Modern Music.*

Books by Douglas Moore

A GUIDE TO MUSICAL STYLES
From Madrigal to Modern Music, Revised Edition

LISTENING TO MUSIC

LISTENING
To Music

by

DOUGLAS MOORE

Revised Edition

The Norton Library
W · W · NORTON & COMPANY · INC ·
NEW YORK

W. W. Norton & Company, Inc. is the publisher of current
or forthcoming books on music by William Austin, Milton Babbitt,
John Backus, Anthony Baines, Sol Berkowitz, Friedrich Blume, How-
ard Boatwright, Nadia Boulanger, Paul Brainard, Nathan Broder,
Manfred Bukofzer, John Castellini, John Clough, Edward T. Cone,
Doda Conrad, Aaron Copland, Hans David, Paul Des Marais, Otto
Erich Deutsch, Frederick Dorian, Alfred Einstein, Gabriel Fontrier,
Walter Gerboth, Harold Gleason, Richard Franko Goldman, Noah
Greenberg, Donald Jay Grout, James Haar, F. Ll. Harrison, Daniel
Heartz, Richard Hoppin, A. J. B. Hutchings, Charles Ives, Roger
Kamien, Hermann Keller, Leo Kraft, Stanley Krebs, Paul Henry
Lang, Jan LaRue, Maurice Lieberman, Irving Lowens, Joseph
Machlis, Carol McClintock, Alfred Mann, W. T. Marrocco, Arthur
Mendel, William J. Mitchell, Douglas Moore, Joel Newman, John
F. Ohl, Carl Parrish, Vincent Persichetti, Marc Pincherle, Walter
Piston, Gustave Reese, Alexander Ringer, Curt Sachs, Arnold Schoen-
berg, Denis Stevens, Robert Stevenson, Oliver Strunk, J. A. Westrup,
Emanuel Winternitz, Walter Wiora, and Percy M. Young.

ISBN 0 393 00130 X

PRINTED IN THE UNITED STATES OF AMERICA

6 7 8 9 0

To Daniel Gregory Mason

CONTENTS

PREFACE

IF AN AUDIENCE EMERGING FROM A CONCERT WERE TO SUBMIT TO
an examination to determine how much of the music had
been understood or even heard we should have an extremely
varied response and probably no perfect papers. Even the
most experienced and sensitive listeners would fall short of
complete appreciation of any music heard for the first time.
Listening to music, which is an art in itself, requires not only
practice but training. Formerly this training was merely a
by-product of other musical studies; today the appreciation of
music is regularly taught in schools and colleges. We are
developing future audiences who will raise the level of music
because they will be able to discriminate between excellence
and mediocrity.

This book is designed to help the lover of music by indicating an approach to its study designed for the listener. No
previous training in music is required to understand the material which it contains. Technical matter is stated as simply
as possible and no technical terms are taken for granted. It
must be remembered, however, that musical experience is the
most important aid to musical appreciation and that the explanations of the text should be related to the music which
they explain. This must be provided by the reader, who with

the aid of a phonograph, radio, or mechanical piano should be able to supplement his opportunities past and present of hearing music.

I am indebted to my colleague, Mr. Bassett W. Hough of the Columbia Department of Music, for many suggestions in preparing this manuscript, also to Professor Margaret E. Maltby of Barnard College for valuable suggestions contained in the chapter on Tone.

DOUGLAS MOORE

Columbia University, 1932.

PREFACE TO REVISED EDITION

THE USE OF THIS BOOK IN CONNECTION WITH MUSIC CLASSES HAS suggested the advisability of certain changes which are now incorporated in the revised edition. The appendix has been enlarged to include specific exercises designed to help the lay student. These exercises, which are based upon the various chapters, are calculated to interest the student and make him participate to a certain extent in actual musical experience. I am indebted for this idea and for other valuable suggestions to Professor Henry G. Pearson of the Massachusetts Institute of Technology. I wish also to thank my colleague, Mr. William Mitchell for assistance in preparing this revision.

For the college student a course in the materials of music based upon this text may profitably be supplemented by the study of Elementary Sight Singing and Musical Notation. As a text book for such study Melville Smith's *Fundamentals of Music,* published by Witmark, is recommended.

The Gramaphone Shop of New York has recently published a new Encyclopedia of Recorded Music which is invaluable in the selection of records for study. All the compositions mentioned in this text are available in recordings.

1937   DOUGLAS MOORE

LISTENING TO MUSIC

CHAPTER I

The Language of Music

NO art is comparable to music in the measure of superiority which the trained feel over the untrained. If you think a poem is a good one and your critical literary friend tells you it is atrocious, your spirits may be momentarily dampened but you will eventually come to the conclusion that after all it is a poem upon a pleasing subject, you like it and that taste is an individual matter anyway. The same comfortable support of your artistic judgment is possible in architecture, painting and sculpture. To begin with, the building or picture does not disappear while the discussion is under way and you can refer to distinctive features of the work at your leisure.

Music, on the other hand, is always disappearing. No sooner have you heard something which gives you a pleasurable or unpleasurable sensation than it has completely evaporated. Not until you have heard a piece so often that you can recall the whole thing and recreate it in your imagination, can you begin to discuss details to support your opinions. Musicians naturally have an advantage in this matter because they are familiar with much more music, and can refer to the notes when in doubt.

But this is not the only feature of music which gives difficulty to the amateur listener. Generally speaking, it is easy to tell what a picture or poem is about or what a building is for, and this makes it possible to follow the thought of the artist. Poetry may be enjoyed in two ways: intellectually by following the development of the author's idea or ideas, and sensuously by perceiving the beauties of sound which it contains. Some people enjoy the intellectual content more, others prefer the so-called music which they find in it, but both pleasures are available to anyone who can read the language in which the poem is written.

The sensuous side of music is available to everyone, trained or untrained. There are very few people who do not enjoy music of one sort or another. It has a great advantage over poetry in that it is a universal language common to all nations.

A large number of listeners to music make no attempt to understand its intellectual content. They accept the pattern of sounds as a relief from the world of reality, allowing themselves to be carried away to some pleasant sphere of fancy where, with the mind relieved of its customary duties, the spirit may be soothed and refreshed.

But is this quite fair to the music? Some of the keenest intellects the world has known have devoted themselves to the composition of music. It would be ridiculous to assume that the art of these composers has nothing to say. To listen to music with a fallow mind is to miss more than half of it because the intellectual and sensuous sides of it are inter-related and interdependent as they are in poetry.

Suppose that you know nothing of Italian and a person with a melodious voice and a good sense of rhythm reads you a symphonic poem, we are told that we are in the interior of a sick room, a man is dying, he struggles for breath; from time to time he thinks of his boyhood, his youth and his loves. A final struggle comes and he dies. The bell tolls his passing. His soul emerges from its earthly encasement and is transfigured. In another symphonic poem, *Till Eulenspiegel,* we are told about a legendary medieval bad boy of Germany. He engages in such pranks as riding on horseback into the midst of the market women, disguising himself as a priest to walk down the street, and hiding in a mouse hole. Eventually he is caught, tried and hanged. If you follow the program carefully you can actually hear him squeal on the gallows.

Berlioz is another composer who furnishes us information about his music. His *Fantastic Symphony* has a weird story which concerns itself with passionate love, a scene at a ball, an opium eater's dream of an execution and finally a witches' sabbath.

Undoubtedly titles and program notes are a very helpful adjunct to the enjoyment of this music. The composers are skilful in describing the events or ideas which they have explained to us in advance. This type of instrumental music is known as program music because its understanding depends upon some story which is furnished us by the composer.

Delightful as program music is and generally easy to follow, there is also a great volume of music about which the composers offer no information. Even the titles convey no idea of the subject matter of the piece. Who knows what the popular *Prelude in C-sharp minor* by Rachmaninoff is about? He has told us nothing. The title simply indicates that it is a short piece in a given key. What would you say to the following program, which some teacher of the Appreciation of Music suggested? "A group of convicts is being paraded to jail in Moscow. The prisoners are exceedingly depressed. At a given signal the guard's attention is diverted, one of them starts to run, others join in the flight, there is an open rebellion and pandemonium in the streets. The soldiers arrive and recapture the prisoners, bind them securely and force them to resume their dismal march. Meanwhile the church-bells toll the victory of law and order." Is this the correct explanation of the *Prelude?* If it is, Rachmaninoff should be prepared to admit it. If he doesn't, we shall have to prove that the lecturer was right by analysing the language of the music. There must be some general principles governing this language which we can learn so that we can analyse things ourselves. We cannot forever be running after lecturers asking them to explain all the music with non-descriptive titles.

Let us take stock and see what idioms of the language we already know. All of us can recognize certain imitations of natural sounds in music. Bells, for instance, hunting horns, guns, thunder, horses' hooves, birds and the buzzing of insects can be almost exactly imitated by the large modern orchestra. It might be well for you to make up a list of imitative sounds which you can actually hear in music. Probably it will be much larger than the above. If you are much of a concert-goer you will not fail to record the bleating of sheep in *Don Quixote* of Strauss, Honegger's locomotive in *Pacific 231* or Gershwin's taxi horns in *An American in Paris*.

When your list is complete and you are certain that you have included only those imitative sounds which you are sure to recognize, test yourself upon the result. You will probably need someone to help you. Let him select records with descriptive titles with which you are unfamiliar, withholding from you any explanatory information. Now as you hear the music, note the various things which you recognize and see if you can guess what the composition is about. If at first you do not get anywhere, try again until you can convince yourself that you do or do not understand this music.

Now for our findings. Did you perhaps mistake thunder for guns and decide that what was supposed to be a battle was for you a storm at sea? Or did you make the lamentable error of thinking the whole thing was a waterfall? If you had known the title you might not have made such a mistake, but we are trying to find out if we can hear the language of music without titles. Obviously either this is a very inexact language or our ears and imaginations are inexpert.

At this point you may protest indignantly. In fact you should, and the greater your irritation, the more promising your future as an intelligent listener to music. We all know that music can imitate sounds, and that such imitation is frequently delightful when encountered in a composition, provided we have been led to expect it by the title. But we find it only in music which sets out to be descriptive, and such music is but a small part of the literature. The language of music is much more abstract. It exists upon a more elevated plane. Story-telling, although it is possible within limitations of great inexactitude and the need of much previous explanation, is not the true purpose of music. The first theme of Beethoven's Fifth Symphony, which he described as "Fate knocking at the door," is not pictorial but abstract. He does not expect us to imagine a hooded figure actually rapping four times on the door. Instead, if anything, he wishes us to understand the overwhelming emotion of a man temporarily crushed by fate.

Almost every great composition is the expression of some emotion. The composer who has experienced this emotion undertakes to communicate it to his audience by his art. This art takes possession of our feelings, captures our imaginations and allows us to share his feeling. Because its language is abstract, music is able to say the unutterable. In *Death and Transfiguration* we feel the solemnity of death, the nostalgia of the past, the glory of resurrection. The story is secondary. Whether or not we follow it, we cannot help feeling these great emotions which Strauss has made so eloquent in the music. For such a language stories are unnecessary, things of the material world are almost an intrusion. That is why the majority of music which we hear is without titles or program. The composer has not wished to hamper our flights of imagination. In the *Prelude* of Rachmaninoff our feeling of sadness and unrest need not be turned into a Moscow anecdote. Story-telling often gets in the way of the pure enjoyment of the emotion which the music suggests.

What of the emotion embodied in the music? Is it exact? Can we learn to identify it without some assistance from the composer? A short time ago an experiment was conducted in a class in psychology at Columbia University. A list of abstractions which music could express was prepared as follows:

1. Exuberance, intoxication
2. Piety, religious devotion
3. Sweetness, loveliness, charm

4. Humor, playfulness, whimsicality
5. Reflectiveness, seriousness
6. Patriotism
7. Sadness, longing, mournfulness
8. Erotic passion
9. Harshness, hardness, cruelty
10. Tranquillity, serenity, calmness
11. Gentleness, mildness
12. Weakness, feebleness
13. Fanaticism, fury
14. Joy, festival
15. Death
16. Despair, frenzied melancholy
17. Mysticism, contemplation
18. Majesty, grandeur
19. Revolution, agitation
20. Love, tenderness

As you read over the list familiar musical examples will occur to you. The last movement of the *Pathetic Symphony* of Tschaikowsky is at once suggested by despair, frenzied melancholy; *Ase's Death,* from the *Peer Gynt* music of Grieg, brings death at once to our minds; the *Marseillaise* is more an expression of revolution than of patriotism. This seems obvious but we must not forget that the titles of these compositions have already communicated some idea of their emotional content to us. We know that the *Marseillaise* actually was a revolutionary hymn which added its share to the downfall of Louis XVI. Can we identify emotions of unfamiliar music without the aid of previous information?

Perhaps you would like to make the experiment yourself. Make your own list of abstractions which you are sure you could recognize. Again let someone play you some music which has a descriptive title without telling you what it is. You will find you have much greater success in this than you had in identifying stories. The moods of a piece of music are often very clear. Yet even in this identification, you will be surprised to find that you are sometimes at variance with the composer.

The results at Columbia were astonishing in their inexactitude. The students participating in this experiment were not trained in music but all of them stated that they were fond of it and went occasionally to concerts. Out of twenty compositions played, in one case only was there substantial agreement as to the underlying emotion. Practically the entire class voted that the choral of Bach, *Now Let Every Tongue Adore Thee,* represented majesty and grandeur; but in the others only the minority agreed with the obvious intention of the composer. For instance the *Golliwog's Cake Walk* of Debussy was voted humorous, as the title would seem to indicate, by five and the other votes were as follows: exuberant five, harsh two, fanatic three, joyful three, despairing one, mystic one and agitated four. The *Hymn to Joy* from the last movement of the Ninth Symphony of Beethoven was identified variously as joy, piety, harshness, exuberance, tranquillity, mysticism, majesty and erotic passion. The *Love Death* from *Tristan and Isolda,* generally conceded to be the most eloquent expression of passionate love ever written, was set down as exuberant, humorous, reflective, sad, weak, fanatic, despairing, majestic and revolutionary, with the addition of a few votes for love.

Would a group of trained musicians do any better with a list of unfamiliar compositions? Probably, because there are certain conventions relating to the expression of emotion which would be of assistance to an experienced listener. Nevertheless these conventions vary from age to age. In the nineteenth century music in a minor mode usually meant sadness, but had no such limitation in earlier times. Perhaps you will recall the old carol *God Rest You Merry Gentlemen* which is in minor. There is no sadness here, but gaiety and good cheer.

If experienced musicians were to take such a test and should do badly in it, they would not be in the least disturbed. They would assure you that they understood the music perfectly and felt its emotional strength but were in no way impelled to label the emotion which they had experienced. After all, why should they? Suppose you experience the sensation of joy when you are walking in the middle of a fragrantly blooming field in spring, with a soft wind bringing you the perfume of the locust blossoms and the sun not too warm but warm enough to reassure your spirit of adventure. Do you at such a time exclaim; "Aha, joy is the emotion I am now experiencing?" If you did, wouldn't such recognition of the emotion tend to lessen its force? When we are deeply moved, we are least prepared to analyse our feelings.

Now let us see what happens to the composer. Something impels him to write a piece of music. He is moved by a beautiful landscape or a poem or a lovely face. He becomes enthusiastic and decides to write something. It may begin with the fragment of a melody or a bit of rhythm singing within him. He may not know what it was that affected him this way, or he may recognize his inspiration and embody it in his composition. In either case he may decide to say nothing in the title which would indicate the source of his inspiration. Why should he? It might be that if he wrote a charming little piece and called it "Golden Rod" many people who heard the piece and recognized the charm of the music would feel that the title interfered with their enjoyment because they didn't feel that way about golden rod. Our feelings are private affairs and we are under no obligation to reveal their source. Music is especially satisfactory because it allows us to enjoy emotion which is indefinite and uncatalogued. Composers vary considerably in their opinions about this. Wagner tells us everything he feels, wants his music illustrated by explicit action and does not hesitate to describe himself and his most personal feelings in his operas. Practically every note of Wagner has a label telling you what inspired it. Brahms on the other hand is reticent about himself. But his music is warm and full of feeling; it may well have been inspired by people and things. Yet he prefers to give you his inspiration without a label. Why not enjoy it in the same way?

Let us agree then that whereas the pictorial side of music is relatively unimportant, the emotional side is important but almost wholly subjective. If we feel that the *Love Death* is despairing, we are right and Wagner is wrong so far as we are concerned. At all events let us listen to the music and enjoy it for what it means to us. But if we adopt such an independent course we shall have to reconsider our ideas about the language of music. In the case of a language so vague, how formulate plans for its study? Should one merely listen passively, as most people do, and enjoy it?

The reason we cannot abandon ourselves to such an agreeable program of auditory indolence is that we shall be back once more in the situation we were in when we listened to Dante's verse without understanding a word of it. For music is a language in which tones are substituted for words, sentences are made out of melodies, and themes become the subject for discussion. Music consists of two principal elements, expression and design. Expression, equally important as design, is nevertheless highly subjective and vague. Design on the other hand is exact and full of meaning. If we do not hear the tones and sense their relation one to another, we are missing the true purport of the music.

Generally speaking our ears are much less disciplined than our eyes, and less responsive. We are taught at an early age to do things with our eyes, to read, to distinguish colors and shapes, and many other feats so usual that they do not seem remarkable. But the cultivation of our ears, after we have accomplished the necessary art of language, we generally neglect. That is unless we study music, which essentially is the science of tone perception and discrimination.

Being a musician does not necessarily mean possessing skill on an instrument. A very unmusical person may acquire considerable facility upon the piano. That delightful instrument has the proper tones all ready for him, supposedly in tune and available to anyone who wants to depress its keys. The singer or violinist has to find his own tones and correct them by his ear. Therefore it is usually wiser to begin the study of music by learning to sing in tune or, failing a voice, to study the violin. When one has acquired a sense of pitch and the ability to remember tones, one may study musical notation, which is only a means of recording music, not music itself. The important thing to remember, for the person who is fond of music but has had no training, is that he can develop the perceptive powers of his ear without knowing how to read notation or learning how to play an instrument. These features of musical training are necessary for the musician but not necessary at all for the intelligent listener. It occasionally happens that a person who has heard a great deal of music but who cannot read music or play an instrument has a more discriminating ear than someone proficient in these arts. Possibly it is because he is not distracted by the purely mechanical processes which reading and playing involve, or his ear may have been better to start with. Ears vary noticeably in their capacities. At any rate the ear may be trained to a high degree of skill by practice in listening to music.

It hardly seems necessary to state that the trained, discriminating ear will find a more intense pleasure in the art than the ear which does not really hear and which admits only a fragment of the musical content of a composition to the consciousness. The important question is how the ambitious listener may receive this training. There is no substitute for practice in listening. The person who from childhood has heard frequent performances of the best music will require no lessons in music appreciation. His ear will have formed habits of listening by instinct. In this golden age when performances of good music are so available and reproductions by phonograph or radio are everywhere at hand, all that is necessary to become an intelligent listener is the will to do so. There are, however, certain conventions about the language of music which may be studied to quicken the interest of the student and focus the attention of the inner ear.

That such study is profitable is easily proved by analogy with another art. Most of us understand the fundamental technical problems of architecture. We know that foundations hold up walls and that there must be balance and adjustment of these if there is to be a roof. But if we wish to enjoy the beauty of design of such an edifice as the cathedral at Chartres, we are willing to prepare ourselves by reading something of the traditional plan of ecclesiastical architecture. We form from this some idea of the relation of aisles to nave, of transept to choir, of buttress to wall. Perhaps we even take the trouble to study the symbolism of medieval glass. If we do, our enjoyment is much greater than that of the careless tourist to whom the cathedral is merely another triple-starred event in Baedeker which must be seen but not necessarily understood.

Some lovers of music feel that the analysis of a composition destroys its beauty, that in listening for details one misses the meaning of the whole. This is true in part. The ideal way to enjoy music is to listen understandingly without conscious effort of attention. We have seen that most of us prefer to listen for the emotional content with only instinct to guide us. We must attempt to train our perceptive faculties so that they also become instinctive. For a time you will find that by concentrating upon details of design you are missing something of the sensuous beauty. Perhaps it would be a good thing to vary your methods of approach. Listen to the first part of a given program with careful attention to detail, trying to impress themes upon your mind and to recall them. Then take a holiday and dream for the last part. You will find that your daydreams will grow less frequent when you begin really to hear the music and to discover delights in it which you never imagined existed.

The purpose of the succeeding chapters will be to introduce your ear to details which can be found in listening to music. You have doubtless encountered in your educational experiences praise for the "seeing eye." Let us now embark in pursuit of the "hearing ear."

CHAPTER II

Musical Tone

ONE man's music is often another man's noise. The highly individual element of taste enters into our judgments so that we usually brand as unmusical the sounds that displease us. The word music has a certain connotation of beauty which we must put aside if we are to get anywhere in our discussion. There may be standards of beauty which can be applied to music, but as in the case of emotional content they are subjective and unrelated to our present study. Still, everyone knows that there is a definite distinction between tone and noise. They both exist in the realm of sound. What exactly is the difference?

We know that sound is caused by disturbances of the atmosphere set in motion by vibrating substances such as membranes, taut strings and the air itself when confined in a hollow tube. The longer, thicker and heavier is the vibrating substance, the fewer the number of vibrations per second and the lower the tone. The shorter, thinner and lighter the vibrating substance, the greater the number of vibrations and the higher the tone.

Musical instruments are not the only agents of tone production. Almost every sound you hear has a recognizable tone or combination of tones. Trained ears can distinguish this tone easily but you will be surprised to discover that by concentration you can do very well yourself. Suppose you sit down quietly and pay attention to the sounds about you. If you are in the country, you will find such agreeable things to listen to as the song of the birds, the buzzing of insects, a distant locomotive, the wind in the trees. If you are in town, your choice may be embarrassingly large, but perhaps you can isolate a bell or two, the hum of a trolley car, or the pneumatic riveter usually to be found next door. Listen to these sounds carefully and see if you can pitch your voice to the approximate tone. If you find difficulty in this, go to the piano and hunt for the tone you hear. If the tone is a combination of sounds like the locomotive whistle, you will not find it so easy but after a few experiments you will discover that many of the sounds which we regard as noises have really a semblance of musical tone.

Now compare this tone with the sound of a fire siren starting with a growl and mounting to a formidable shriek. You may be able to imitate this, but you certainly cannot pitch your voice to any particular tone which resembles it. In fact it seems to have no tone at all but is simply noise. Here is the fundamental distinction between tone and noise. When the vibrations are constant and unwavering we have tone, when they are intermittent and variable, we have noise.

Physicists tell us that there are 11,000 tones which our ears can differentiate. The highest vibrates at the rate of 38,000 per second, the lowest at 16. Such a number of tones is far too great for use in music. The inexpert ear has enough difficulty in distinguishing between the approximate 90 that we use in our Western system of tone. Music is a comparatively young art and as it increases in complexity more tones may be called into service. There is a tendency today among certain modern composers to split the distances between tones so as to admit new ones, but for our study of traditional musical organization, we shall find that practically all the tones which we need are to be found on the piano, usually 88 counting both white and black keys.

The traditional tones inherited from the Greeks upon which our system is built are represented approximately by the white keys on the piano. It is interesting to speculate how these tones were originally established. Without delving into ancient musical history it is safe to assume that they were adopted after centuries of painful experimentation and long efforts of standardization. The tones of the Greeks were really one of the great discoveries of the history of civilization.

Why not try a little experimenting yourself? Pitch your voice upon any tone that occurs to you and sing upward tone by tone. After a few sounds you will arrive upon a tone which seems like the completion of the cycle, a duplicate of the first except that it is higher in pitch. In the same way, we discover that there is a tone below our starting point identical in character except that it is lower in pitch. This relationship of periodically similar tones which occur as the pitch is raised or lowered is called the *octave*. Practically all systems of music are based upon the octave relationship. Now sing from your original note up to its octave and count how many tones you sang in all. Were there eight or thirteen? If you sang eight you were probably singing the tones of the Greeks. If you sang thirteen, you may have included the extra tones which we have gradually added to enrich our system.

If you examine the keyboard of the piano, you will find that the distinction between the original and added tones of our system is very clear; the former are represented by the white keys, the latter by the black.

You will furthermore observe from the topography of the keyboard that the black notes alternate in groups of two and three allowing for regularly repeating groups of white notes. If you start with any note in the low register and look for the next one above it, similarly located, you will find that it sounds an octave higher. The piano of normal size keyboard is divided into seven and a third octaves. From the above diagram you will see that tones which are similarly located and which sound alike also have the same letter name.

Suppose you select the tone of C which is in about the center of the keyboard and play upward to the octave using the white notes. This succession of sounds suggests the familiar scale which at some point of our education we have either been taught to sing or play. Did it ever occur to you that this scale which seems so natural to us is rather eccentric because all the tones in it are not an equal distance apart? Look at the keyboard and you will see that between the third and fourth note or E and F there is no black key providing for intermediate tone, nor is there any to be found between the seventh note B and the octave. The interval between E and F and between B and C is the same as the interval between C and the black note above it. By *interval* is meant the ratio of the number of vibrations of the higher tone to that of the lower. If you were able to count the number of vibrations, you would find this ratio exactly the same. The piano is conveniently divided into 88 tones which are an equal interval apart counting both white and black notes. In our system we call this interval between tones a *half tone.* The interval between C and D which have a black note between them is therefore that of a *whole tone,* but between E and F and B and C where the black key is missing, the interval is only that of a half tone.

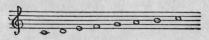

MAJOR SCALE ON C

The familiar scale upon which practically all of our music is based consists of a rising series of seven tones and their duplications in octaves. The interval between each of these tones is as follows (using C as point of departure):

1 and 2 (*C and D*) whole tone
2 and 3 (*D and E*) whole tone
3 and 4 (*E and F*) half tone
4 and 5 (*F and G*) whole tone
5 and 6 (*G and A*) whole tone
6 and 7 (*A and B*) whole tone
7 and 8 (*B and C*) half tone

This relationship seems very arbitrary, although it has so long existed that we might never be tempted to question it.

Probably it could be explained in terms of the experiments of Pythagoras in the sixth century B. C. According to Pole, the English musical scholar, the relationship of the octave was understood before the time of Pythagoras, but there was much confusion about the number and pitch of the intermediate tones. It was his experiments of the numerical relationships of tones which contributed to the establishment of the tonal sub-divisions of the octave that we have included in our system.

Pythagoras started his experiments with a taut string which sounded E. He divided this string into two parts and found that one-half its length, when sounded alone, gave E the octave above. He next divided the string into three equal parts and found that two-thirds its length gave the tone of B which, you will observe, is the fifth note if you play a rising series of white notes on the piano keyboard starting with E. Three-quarters of the length of the original string gave him A, or the fourth note in the series we have just examined. He decided that because the numerical relationship of these tones was logical and simple, they formed the proper division of the octave and that the distance between them should be regarded as a tone. Counting down from the A to the E and up from the B to the E above and measuring in terms of this newly determined "tone" he found the interval the same in each case, two tones and something over which was nearly half a tone in extent. This remainder he called a *hemitone,* later known as a *semitone* or *half tone.* It was in this fashion that the natural relationship of tones to half tones was established.

Each octave then, counting the note of departure and the

note of arrival, consists of eight tones, two pairs of which are a semitone apart. The position of the half tones will be determined by the note of departure. Pythagoras did not prescribe the arrangement which we know as the major scale. The Greeks used scales starting on several different tones and only incidentally the one on C. What he did give us is the division of tones within the octave and this relationship has remained fairly constant since his discoveries.

If you are curious about the effect upon melodies of the different scales used by the Greeks and also in the Middle Ages, you can experiment by picking out familiar tunes at the piano keyboard using only white notes and starting upon a degree that will not call for the C major scale. For instance try *My Country 'Tis of Thee* commencing upon G and see how far you will get without striking a white note which seems definitely wrong. You will find it to be F and will prefer to correct it by playing F sharp, the black key immediately above it. Try it again, however, without the correction and see if the unfamiliar effect produced by the melody does not give you a new and agreeable sensation suggesting a melody which might perhaps be very old. That sensation is caused by the fact that with the F instead of the F sharp you have lowered the seventh degree of your customary scale so that the half step comes at a place where you do not expect it. Some old hymns still sung in church services are based upon the old scales; a good example of one of them is *Oh Come, Oh Come Emmanuel*. Very old folk songs often contain turns of the melody which suggest the old scales. These scales are usually referred to as the antique modes as distinct from our major and minor scales.

OH COME, OH COME EMMANUEL
(AEOLIAN MODE)

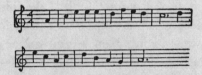

Notice that you could correct the version of *America* played on G by using F sharp instead of F. That explains one of the reasons why we have added to our system the tones represented by the black notes. When musicians began to favor the scale represented by the white note progression on C, they often found that the melody would lie too high or too low for comfort and sought to reproduce it at a higher or lower level, but not one so far removed as the octave. Accordingly to reproduce the required whole and half step relationship necessary for this scale, new tones were needed, half steps between some of the other tones. The result was the gradual evolution of an octave divided into 13 tones (counting extremes) instead of 8. With these 13 tones or 12 without the octave duplication we can produce our major scale commencing upon any degree.

If you want to experiment at the keyboard, you can yourself find the major scale starting from any degree. Remember that you want a half tone between the third and fourth degree and the seventh and eighth, that the piano is divided into semitones and that you must progress to the degree which will give you the proper interval. With regard to sharps and flats and the names of the notes, a rule that will work quite consistently is that there must be a different letter for each note of the scale and that they must always move alphabetically. On the piano F sharp is the same as G flat, but in the scale of D, the names will naturally run D E F sharp for you couldn't skip from E to G flat with no F at all. In the scale of D flat, this note will be G flat and you will have D flat, E flat, F, G flat. It couldn't be F sharp for you have used up the letter F. You may be confused when you get on some degrees to find that sharps and flats are not always black notes, that C appears as B sharp in the series starting on C sharp, or that you may even resort to the expression double sharp or double flat in some of the extreme keys in order to have your nomenclature consistent.

The piano is a very useful instrument. It can play many tones at once in contrast to the voice and many other instruments which can produce only one tone at a time. Also if it is in tune, it will give you the proper tone without any effort on your part save the purely mechanical one of depressing a key. Each key has one or more strings fashioned in the correct length to produce the necessary vibrations for each of the tones that we use. These strings are subject to atmospheric conditions; from time to time they have to be corrected by a tuner who must have a very good ear in order to regulate them. But in striking a note on the piano, your ear plays no part. The tone is ready made. This is both an advantage and a disadvantage. It allows the performer with an inaccurate ear to play in tune, whereas the same person might be unable to pitch his voice satisfactorily or sing accurately. But the piano cannot slide from one note to another as we have seen the voice can do. Between each note on the piano there is a great space of tone which it cannot record. The voice is able to pass from one tone to another with a gradual raising or lowering of pitch so that this intervening space may be felt. There is a great sea of tone in which the tones which the piano plays are only small islands. Here is the great difference between an upward motion on the piano and the fire siren. The fire siren goes through the whole sea of tone, stopping nowhere, with no point of focus, giving the effect of noise. The piano moves upward or downward, tone by tone, passing gracefully from familiar island to familiar island. There is no doubt that our ears are overwhelmed by the whole sea of tone. It confuses us and leaves us with no definite tonal impression. We like our familiar islands and the less that we hear of the intervening space, the better for our peace of mind. That is why, when a piano is out of tune or someone sings off pitch, we are distressed. How many times we have felt unhappy when a singer reaching for a high note runs short of breath and does not provide the note with enough vibrations to produce it in tune. He or she does not sing another recognizable tone; it is merely a debased version of the one we have been expecting, not safely on the island. You may have heard the expression "the middle of the tone." That means that the player must be careful not to skirt the edges and make the tone a shade too high or too low but must arrive in the very center of the island well out of the disturbing sea.

Now comes a very curious feature about our tones and their relationship. Did you happen to notice, when you were trying to identify the tone of one of the natural sounds to which you listened, that you could sing it correctly but when you went to the piano it did not precisely fit any note that you found there? Your voice appeared to be on a perfectly recognizable island which did not exist on the piano. Or did you ever notice that when two pianos both in tune were played together they did not agree? How can this be in a definite system based upon only twelve tones and their duplicates in octaves? The answer is that pitch, which determines tones, is relative. Our tones may be accurately produced starting from any definite number of vibrations as a point of departure. The relationships of our system of tones, as we have seen, are determined by fixed ratios. In the history of pitch the standard of tuning varies widely with a tendency to rise. Tuning is generally regulated with A as a point of departure, that is the A in the middle register of a woman's voice. We have today what we call *concert pitch,* which means that A is tuned to 440 vibrations per second. All other notes are tuned relative to this. And yet A in the past has been tuned as low as 415. That would be much nearer A flat than A and yet if you were to hear a piano tuned to A at 415 with no opportunity for comparison with another tuned to concert pitch, you probably would not notice the difference. Some people have a sense of pitch so accurate that they can tell the exact pitch of a tone without comparing it with any other. They will tell you what note you have sung or what note you have struck merely by the sound of it. They can tell at once if an instrument is tuned too high or too low. This faculty, called *absolute pitch,* is rather rare even among musicians although by long practice it may be acquired approximately.

The fact that we accept such a wide latitude in point of departure for our tuning does not seem to reconcile itself at all with our distrust of tones beyond our islands of safety. Our sense of pitch is entirely relative and yet once we have adopted a standard we do not like any variation. The reason for this is probably auditory laziness. Our minds never accept additional problems without a struggle. We are willing to concern ourselves with twelve tones and their duplicates but we have a noticeable disinclination to bother with any others. The fact that we can hear many additional tones is proved by the complacency with which we accept all the tones of two pianos tuned almost a half tone apart. It is within the realm of possibility that we might expand our capacity for additional tonal relationships.

There are undoubtedly many tonal islands which we could perceive if we cared to make the effort. Try to sing a quarter tone: sing a half tone and then go from one degree to the other and see if you can focus upon an intermediate tone.

Recently a piano has been devised which can play quarter tones. Two adjacent keyboards are used, one tuned at the interval of a quarter tone below the other. The piano, which has exerted a tremendous influence over music during the last hundred years, is one of the principal bulwarks against the adoption of quarter tones. Perhaps if quarter-tone pianos become widely adopted, our ears will abandon their inertia and welcome more additions to our tonal system.

Now let us glance at the violin which is much nearer to the potentialities of the human voice than the piano. It employs four strings which are tuned generally to agree with whatever piano happens to be at hand. These strings do not stay in tune for long periods as do those of the piano. They must be corrected by the performer each time before he plays and sometimes even between pieces. When they are in tune, the violinist can play four notes, G, D, A and E. It would be a very meagre supply of tones upon which to make music if he confined himself to these. Imagine a performer playing the instrument. The neck of the instrument rests in his left hand, the base is supported by his chin and shoulder. With his right hand he holds the bow which drawn across the strings excites them to vibrate. But have you noticed what he does with the fingers of his left hand? They are continually moving about on the strings, not striking them but by pressure shortening the length of the string which is vibrating, thereby producing a higher tone. How does he know where to depress the string so that the higher tone that he wants will be exact? The mandolin, guitar and banjo have frets on the finger board. If the string is depressed midway between two frets the middle of the required tone will be achieved. But there are no frets on the violin, nothing to indicate our islands of safety. The violinist must learn by means of an accurate coördination between fingers and ear exactly what the proper spots are. When he is in an early stage of his technical development, he sometimes resorts to the trial and error method, producing a tone near the one he wants and then correcting by sliding. This sliding is very disagreeable to our ears because it destroys our sense of tonal security. We like our violinists best in an advanced stage of technical maturity where they will guide us about from island to island without too much swimming to shore.

Now notice his left hand again as his fingers select the notes. Does it appear calm and still or does it tend to wobble? At times it seems to be rocking slightly especially when the tone he is producing is very beautiful. The consequent movement of the surface of the finger on the string must be altering the tone slightly. It is; and what we are hearing is the violinist's *vibrato*. If he plays without vibrato the tone is rather dull. What he accomplishes by this motion is a slight shading of tone moving constantly from the under edge of the tone into the middle of it. It seems curious that we should prefer this to a steady production of the middle of the tone. Again the explanation is that it is habit. We have come to like this slight wavering of pitch on the violin and the tone so produced sounds more expressive to our ears. This is another proof that our ears are capable of appreciating more tones than we realize. Ask a violinist to play a note first without and then with vibrato. You will notice the difference at once and will prefer the latter tone. Now ask him to vibrate above as well as below the tone, producing the exaggerated effect that circus performers think the public likes. You will see that this is less good because it turns a sound which is subtly interesting to something obvious and cheap. If the violinist vibrates too far afield he will give the effect of a *trill* or two notes sounded back and forth in rapid succession. This is agreeable but naturally produces an entirely different effect from the normal vibrato.

Ask the violinist to slide his finger up and down the string while playing. Again the fire siren. We have the sea of tone without any points of focus. Sometimes the violinist uses this effect which is called *portamento*. It gives us somewhat the feeling that we have when we are in an elevator which drops suddenly beneath us. Many people like this sensation. At any rate the effect must be used with discretion.

There is a distinct tendency toward portamento today,

chiefly to be found in our dance music. Perhaps it is because our ears are getting more familiar with the sea of tone, or possibly it is merely the elevator motif expressing itself again. The "waw-waw" sliding type of singing is just now very popular. Radio "crooners" seldom go from the middle of one tone to the middle of another in a way that we should describe as clean singing. They scoop about, traversing large unfamiliar tonal areas, thereby causing considerable excitement and pleasure to the ears of their more impressionable hearers. The slide trombone, which is an expert at portamento, is naturally popular in the dance orchestra. Whether the tendency to blur the relationship of one tone to another is a forward or a backward step is an open question. Among the savages where musical expression and sensibility is not very highly developed, we find the same tonal blurring and consequent inability to focus upon clear tone. Some of our modern composers find this very stimulating and try to imitate it. Art is said to move in cycles. Perhaps we are merely on the other side of the circle from our ancestors of the eighteenth and nineteenth centuries who sought to make tonal relationships more distinct.

If you are of an adventurous mind and would like to explore some of the unfamiliar tonal sea, expose yourself to some oriental music. The systems upon which the music of China, India and Java is based are entirely different from our own. Musicians of these nations use not only different scales but different tonal relationships. Many of their scales use the smaller interval of the quarter tone to which the Asiatic ears are perfectly accustomed. The result to our ears is unfamiliarity which is so great that we think oriental music lacking in variety and rather discordant. This is precisely the impression which the orientals form from our music except that they find in ours an additional disadvantage. To them our tones are too far apart. They miss the quarter tone intervals and find our music full of holes. It is excellent training for the Western ear to listen to their music and try to follow it. After you have become familiar with a piece of oriental music, you may discover that it has variety, tonal definiteness and possibly considerable charm. Perhaps some day the various systems will unite. Certainly the oriental music is exerting an influence today upon our experimentally-minded composers and Western music is increasingly heard in the East.

So much for the pitch of our musical tones and what distinguishes them from noise. There are two more peculiarities of tone which we must consider. Why is it that one tone is louder than another and why do two instruments playing tones of exactly the same pitch sound so different? The first question is easy to understand. Loudness of tone depends upon what physicists call *amplitude* of vibrations. When the tone is excited with greater force, the resulting sound waves are wider in extent and there will be correspondingly greater stimulation of the auditory nerve. If the violinist bears down heavily upon his bow, the singer uses a greater amount of breath or the pianist strikes the piano a more forceful blow, the amplitude rather than the number of the vibrations is affected. It sometimes happens in wind instruments that greater pressure of air will cause the tone to rise, but this is only after a certain point of loudness has been reached. The French horn can produce notes which we call overblown.

The performer uses the key for the tone below and sends such a current of air through the instrument that not only is the amplitude of vibrations affected but their number increased.

Characteristic tone color of instruments is a much more difficult problem. It is easy to see that method of excitation of the sound will affect the color of it. A note produced by scraping a string with a bow will differ from a note produced by blowing through a tube or striking a taut string by a hammer. But this does not tell us why two voices sound noticeably different, or why the clarinet and the oboe, both instruments made of wood with vibrating reeds, are nothing alike. What is it that makes one A with its 440 vibrations sound entirely different from another A with precisely the same number?

Many theoretical explanations have been advanced by scientists, but the one most generally accepted is that of the German scientist, Helmholtz. He attributes the difference in color of tones to the presence or absence of *harmonics* or *upper partials*. Every sound that we hear is not a single sound but a complex tone made up of various contributing factors. This is caused by the fact that each sounding body vibrates not only along its entire length but in segments as well. While the principal system of vibration is proceeding along the entire length, the two halves of the body are vibrating simultaneously and contributing to the resultant tone. Also the thirds, quarters, fourths, fifths and so on *ad infinitum* are vibrating as well. It is easy to calculate the sounds that these partial vibrations are making if we know the length of the main vibrating substance. They have a relationship which is constant. The first harmonic of any main or fundamental sound is the octave above. The second one is five notes above this, the third two octaves above the fundamental, the fourth three notes higher than this and so on until our ear can no longer discover them.

HARMONICS

A good experiment to prove to yourself the reality of harmonics is this: depress the C an octave below middle C on the keyboard so that the felt is held off the string, allowing it to vibrate if so impelled; but do not excite the vibration by striking the note. Now strike the C above which is the first harmonic, immediately releasing the key. The sound of it seems to persist although the only undampened string is the low C. What has happened is that the actual striking of the first harmonic has caused the partial tone of the fundamental to be excited sympathetically. You can repeat this experiment satisfactorily by sounding each of the natural harmonics in succession. If you are skeptical, try some of the notes out of the system; you will find that their sound does not persist for an instant.

A violinist can show you harmonics very readily. By touching the middle of the string lightly he can cause only half of it to vibrate, producing an eerie sound like a soft whistle. Harmonics play an important part in the music of all stringed instruments, because they give an added resource to the performer.

The theory of Helmholtz is that these partial tones vary in prominence and intensity in each of the different instruments. The quality of the tone is due to the number and strength of the partials sounding. The flute, for instance, the tone of which is so pure, permits few upper partials to sound; the oboe, the reedy quality of which is in direct contrast to the flute, has strong partials, particularly the higher ones. The clarinet's tone, which is somewhat opaque, is richer in its odd numbered partials than even. Chimes are very rich in partial tones (even including tones outside of our system of islands); these sound so clearly that we sometimes find it hard to distinguish the fundamental tone. Perhaps you have heard a pianist imitate the sound of chimes. He does this by playing, in addition to the fundamental tones, some of the harmonics. The astonishingly good effect of chimes which can be produced upon the piano is an interesting corroboration of the Helmholtz theory of tone color.

Further proof is offered by certain other experiments in sound. In the laboratories of the Bell Telephone Company instruments have been perfected which can isolate partials from fundamental tone and from each other. Some records have been issued which show the effect upon the tone of various musical instruments by tampering with harmonics. For example, the tone of a given note upon the piano, the horn and the cello when upper partials have been eliminated is almost precisely similar and amazingly hard to differentiate. As the partials are added one by one, the tone of the instrument takes on its characteristic color.

Large organs contain what are known as *mixture stops*. These are control pipes which do not sound the note depressed but a given harmonic of it. When many other pipes are sounding the fundamental, this harmonic gives brilliance to the tone by strengthening an upper partial which is already sounding. The tone which the mixture pipe is playing merges into the fundamental tone and loses its identity. Many French and German organs in the great cathedrals contain a great number of mixture stops, a fact which accounts for their somewhat nasal brilliance when sounding the full organ.

So much for the physical properties of tone: pitch, volume and color. The student of physics will undoubtedly possess more information upon the subject than is necessary to include here. What interests us particularly is to force our ears to listen attentively to sounds so that we can begin to discover subtleties of tonal shading that we never knew existed. We arrive after much effort of careful listening at the conclusion that the distinction between noise and tone is less great than we imagined, and that our system of musical tone, rich and fertile as it is, is capable of still greater development.

CHAPTER III

The Agencies of Musical Tone

A PIECE of music must pass through several important processes before the thought of the composer reaches our minds. In the first place he must develop and arrange his ideas, select the proper vehicle to display the tones which he has imagined, and record the result in musical notation. Let us suppose that it is a piece for piano. The first stage it has undergone is composition. Inspiration, knowledge of musical form, instrumentation and notation have all contributed to the result. Now the music must be performed by someone with skill on the proper instrument and the ability to read musical notation. His performance must be accurate in execution of the notes and in interpretation of the spirit of the work. If it is not, we shall not be in entire communication with the thought of the composer. Finally our ears have the difficult task of selecting and transmitting the tones to our consciousness which in turn must construct them into a complete image and relate them to past musical experiences.

There is an additional step to be taken in some of the music which we hear today. Before our ears receive performances of so-called mechanical music, it must be relayed through the air via the radio, or recorded on disc or roll for the phonograph or player piano. Here is an excellent chance for a misstep. Much good music may fall short of its purpose because of some mechanical imperfection of the relaying instrument. It is undoubtedly safer and more agreeable to be within earshot of the performing artist. There is something of a psychological nature which occurs when music is performed, and which no machinery has yet been able to relay. Just what this is, it is impossible to explain scientifically. Radio and phonograph manufacturers scoff at the idea and say that television will supply the missing quality which they believe to be ocular, not auditory. Perhaps they are right, and they are perfectly fair in calling our attention to the fact that some expert musicians have been unable to distinguish between performances of a pianist and of a mechanical piano of the modern variety when a screen shut out the evidence of their eyes. Nevertheless there is something which is missing even in the best mechanical music. In any case let us be grateful for the rich resources of music which the machine age has brought to our ears. While not the equivalent of the real thing, they are a consoling substitute when we find the real thing inaccessible.

Let us examine a piece of music intended for the piano. Why did the composer write it for piano? Why not for orchestra or for organ? He surely did not use the piano merely because there was one nearby upon which he could fish out his sounds. His trained imagination probably heard all the sounds before a note was played. That is lucky, for if he had been impelled to write a piece for orchestra how would he have tried that over in the privacy of his study? Would the piece have been the same if it had been conceived for orchestra as it is, designed for piano? Possibly so far as the theoretical tones are concerned, certainly not in the actual sounds. Tones have two aspects in their relationship: the *theoretical,* which concerns such things as agreeableness of succession, combination and development; and the *actual,* which must take into account the individual peculiarities of the instruments which embody them. The composer therefore must consider carefully the suitability of the medium through which he is to present his ideas.

Do these mediums vary sufficiently to warrant his and our attention to this element of music? Let us consider the tone of middle C on the piano. Strike it and try to recall the sound in your mind. Now imagine how that same tone would sound on the violin or on the trumpet. Quite different, isn't it? Probably the difference is caused because the piano C is struck by a hammer, the violin C by scraping with horsehair on a string and the trumpet C by blowing in a brass tube. Let us glance at the principal agencies of musical tone.

To begin with there is the human voice, a complicated and sensitive instrument requiring very expert treatment both upon the part of the composer and of the performer. Whether used singly or in chorus, with or without accompaniment, the voice has definite preferences as to the sort of music it likes to perform. We have all of us probably sung enough to realize certain of these peculiarities. For instance we like to sing melodies that do not contain too many skips, that make sparing use of the upper and lower extremities of range, that do not move too swiftly, that have their climaxes in the upper rather than the lower range, that give us a chance to breathe occasionally, for the lungs which supply the wind power can sustain a tone only for a certain length of time. Certain composers write much more agreeably for the voice than certain others. Take Handel for instance. His music is so well conceived for the voice that it almost seems to sing itself. His choral music is infinitely easier and therefore usually more effective in performance than that of Bach who writes less gratefully for the voice. The greatest master of choral writing was Palestrina, who inherited a fertile tradition of choral style. His music seems almost to soothe and rest the voice, so perfectly is it conceived in terms of the vocal organ. When ungrateful or difficult music is attempted by the chorus or a single voice, the tone begins to suffer and the pitch generally wavers disagreeably and falls.

The limitations of the voice are well within the sphere of our own experience; but what of the wealth of instruments which play our music for us? Here is a list of the more familiar ones, classified according to the three main types, string, wind, and percussion. Each class is again divided according to the method of sound production.

I. STRINGED INSTRUMENTS

Instruments which are struck:

PIANO	CYMBALUM	CLAVICHORD (*obsolete*)

Instruments which are bowed:

VIOLIN	VIOLA	VIOLONCELLO	BASS

CORRESPONDING VIOL FAMILY (*obsolete*)

Instruments which are plucked:

HARP	MANDOLIN	GUITAR	BANJO
UKELELE	LUTE (*obsolete*)		HARPSICHORD (*rare*)

II. WIND INSTRUMENTS

Instruments in which the wind vibrates in a hollow tube:

FLUTE   PICCOLO   ORDINARY PIPES OF THE ORGAN

Instruments in which a single reed causes vibration:

CLARINET   BASS CLARINET   SAXOPHONE   REED PIPES OF ORGAN

Instruments in which a double reed causes vibration:

OBOE   ENGLISH HORN   BASSOON   CONTRA BASSOON

Instruments in which elastic membranes set in vibration a column of air (Lips in a mouthpiece):

TRUMPET   FRENCH HORN   TROMBONE   TUBA

III. PERCUSSION INSTRUMENTS

Instruments of indefinite pitch:

SIDE DRUM   BASS DRUM   GONG OR TAM TAM
TRIANGLE   CYMBALS   TAMBOURINE   CASTANETS

Instruments of definite pitch:

ORCHESTRA BELLS (glockenspiel)   XYLOPHONE   CELESTA
BELLS (chimes)   KETTLE DRUM   (PIANO)

You might ask yourself how familiar you are with these instruments. How many of them can you recall now as you try to imagine the individual tone color of each? There are many ways in which you can learn to recognize them. The best method is to go to orchestral concerts and watch as well as listen. The Educational Department of the Victor Talking Machine Company has published an excellent series of charts picturing the instruments of the orchestra as well as records of the characteristic tone color of each of them. If only to sharpen your ear to the subtleties of musical sound, you should learn to distinguish between them all.

We have already seen that the characteristic quality of tone depends upon the upper partials sounding. These are governed by the size and shape of the instrument and the method of exciting the vibrations. As the tone of the instruments varies so do their capabilities and preferences.

Let us imagine again the tone of middle C on several familiar instruments; the piano, organ, flute, harp, trombone and kettle drum. Unfortunately, although our imagination may supply this note on the kettle drum, the instrument cannot, because it is above its playing range. How does it lie on the other instruments? It is about in the middle of the piano, organ and harp; on most flutes it is the lowest possible note; it is a fairly high one on the trombone. Instruments usually have strong and weak registers which must be taken into account in writing for them. There are other differences which we notice in these various Cs. How long will the note of the piano continue to sound after it is struck? The vibrations will die rapidly away after the initial explosion of sound. Compare the C on the organ; it will go on sounding so long as you keep the key depressed. The harp note will die away as will that of the piano, but the flute and trombone will keep on sounding until the performer runs out of breath. How much of a rhythmic accent could each instrument give? The piano best of all; the harder we strike, the louder the note. The harp likewise can make one note stand out above others by force of plucking. Blowing harder on the flute or trombone will produce an accent but it will not be as effective as the one on the piano which is almost as good as a drum beat. How about the C on the organ? Is it possible by striking the key harder to force more wind into the pipe? Unfortunately not; no accent whatever is possible on the organ. How about repeating the note, will its speed of articulation vary? The piano note can be repeated as fast as our fingers will move; so can the note on the organ and the note on the harp. The flute would prefer to articulate rapidly in a higher register, but once there, it can almost hold its own with the piano. The trombone will come off very badly in this matter. He will repeat the note if you wish, but do not ask him to do it too rapidly. How many notes can each of these instruments play at a time? The piano, harp and organ will oblige with as many as you have fingers or other parts of your body to use for striking the keys or plucking the strings. The flute can sound only one note at a time and that is all to be expected from the trombone.

We can see, therefore, that each instrument differs from every other in certain qualities which are bound to have an influence upon the music which it plays. Following is a table of some of the most important instruments showing the differences in compass, variety of strength of a single note, accent value, survival value, speed of articulation for a repeated note and how many notes each instrument can play at once. Calculations are based on a scale of one to ten.

In the table range is only approximate for it depends in the case of some instruments upon the skill of the performer. One kettle drum could not produce the range of thirteen notes. In the orchestra two or more are used. In the case of strength soft to loud, position of the note in the instrument's register will contribute to the result. These calculations are based upon medium register. Survival value depends in the violin upon the length of the stroke of the bow. To produce

Instrument	Compass (Calculated in Semitones)	Strength (Soft to Loud)	Accent Value	Survival Value	Articulation (Repeated Tone)	Notes at a Time
PIANO	88 notes	2–8	10	1	9	all
ORGAN	61 keys manuals 32 keys pedals	1–10	0	10 plus	9	all
VIOLIN	44 notes (exclusive of harmonics)	1–7	8	10	10	4
FLUTE	37 notes	1–5	3	7	9	1
OBOE	33 notes	3–7	5	8 plus	7	1
CLARINET	42 notes	1–7	4	8	7	1
HORN	43 notes	2–10	9	8	8	1
TRUMPET	31 notes	3–10	9	7	8	1
2 KETTLE DRUMS	13 notes	1–10	10	1	5 (any faster articulation gives effect of trill)	2
HARP	82 notes	2–4	7	1	8	49

a soft note this stroke may be considerably prolonged; when the player changes from the down to the up stroke, there will be a scarcely noticeable break. Survival value in other instruments often depends upon volume of tone. The range of the organ may be extended by the use of stops of 4, 2, and 1 foot pitch above and 16 and 32 foot pitch below. Some of the pedal tones duplicate those of the manuals.

The peculiarities and limitations of the instruments are more a problem for the composer and the performer than they are for the listener. Yet if we take the trouble to consider them in their relationship to music, we shall discover a number of interesting facts. For instance what instruments would be best fitted to play an expressive melody? The horn will be better than the trumpet because it has greater range, can play more softly, accent as well, has greater survival value and an equal speed of articulation. The violin, which is also able to play more softly and has a still greater survival value, is likewise a better instrument for a melody than a trumpet. How about the piano? It seems very weak in one important respect, survival value. Each note on the piano is in the nature of an explosion. The maximum tone comes as the note is struck but the vibrations begin to die rapidly away, even if by keeping the key depressed the felt designed to stop the tone is still suspended. In a slow succession of notes on the piano, there is a definite dying away of tone between them. Compare the effect of a melody on the violin or horn. The tone may persist in full until the next note is reached. This makes a much more beautiful effect, for the succession of tones is equalized and the melody is much smoother. Try the experiment yourself. The human voice is like the violin or the horn in survival value. Pick out a simple melody by ear on the piano. Suppose you take *Old Black Joe,* which is slow and expressive. Start on C and you will not have much difficulty if you let your ear serve as guide. When you have found the notes so that the effect is smooth, play the melody as expressively as possible. Now sing it to the best of your ability and compare the result. Do you notice that on the piano the long note on G, the fourth one in the melody, is dying away before you are ready to go on? Suppose you wanted for the sake of expression to have this note grow louder rather than diminish? This is a very common effect in a melody. You can easily achieve this result by singing if you care to try it. But the unfortunate piano is doomed to become softer as the note persists. Paderewski himself could not do anything about this. The composer could, however. He knows that this note will become softer because of the nature of the instrument and if he is to have a pause at this point and his melody wishes to increase in tone, he will have to repeat the note several times, striking it harder each time. This will cause the tone to increase, but you can easily see it is a very inaccurate substitute for the swelling of tone which the wind or bowed instrument can accomplish.

How about a melody on the organ as compared with one on the violin or the piano? We have no trouble here with tone survival. The organ could play a melody of such slow notes that we could take a short nap on each before the arrival of another and still the tone would not diminish between them. We might expect that this fine resource of the instrument would be used to advantage in organ music, and it is. If you will recall the sound of some organ music, you will realize that what you like best about the instrument is the sustained quality of its tone. This gives it a dignity well suited to the needs of religious services. Have you noticed though that a melody on the organ sometimes sounds rather dull as compared to one on the violin or the piano? Why should this be? We can obtain the swelling of tone which the piano could not give to a single note. This is achieved by putting part of the organ in a box with movable shutters. As these shutters are opened or shut by means of the so-called swell pedal, the tone can be made to increase or decrease. But how about the accents of melodies which make one note more important than another by stressing it slightly, which give the needed life and variety to the music? Look at the chart and you will learn the guilty secret of the organ. "Accent value, none." There is no way by which in a given set of pipes one note can be made to have more stress than another. We can increase the tone suddenly by the swell pedal or by drawing another stop, but this will not give us the accent that is so easy for the piano and the violin. As a result melodies on the organ unless they are especially calculated to minimize this defect sound less well than they do on the violin and the horn. This also explains why jazz is so unsatisfactory when played on the organ. To begin with, jazz makes no use of the sustained tone which is the genius of the instrument, but sputters away in short equally stressed notes which the synthetic accents of the swell pedal and stop drawing of the moving picture organists can hardly conceal. Let us admit that the violin and the horn are more useful melodic instruments than the piano and the organ. The piano has difficulty in sustaining tone and the organ in making accents.

How do the instruments compare in rhythm? After what we have learned about accents on the organ, we shall see at once that the organ is the weakest of all instruments rhythmically because inequality of accent is the life of rhythm. Likewise the piano, which is almost as much a percussion instrument as the drum, will be rhythmically very effective. This is why dance music sounds so well on the piano. The violin and the horn however are strong in accent value and are instruments of great rhythmic importance, hardly comparable to the piano, but needing no apologies.

If the violin and the horn are better than the piano and the organ melodically and almost as good as the piano rhythmically, what is the particular virtue of the piano which makes it the most popular of all instruments? The answer is to be found in the last column. How many notes can the instrument sound at once? Here the keyboard instruments win the race and the wind and bowed instruments are nowhere. That is, the bowed instruments are almost nowhere for the violin can play four notes at once by virtue of making a bow stroke across all four strings, but they do not sound exactly together because of the curve of the bridge. Also we are asking our violinist to find four notes with his left hand instead of only one. Perhaps you have noticed that when a violinist plays two or more notes at once, his intonation sometimes becomes shaky unless he is a skilful performer. Double-stopping is very popular in violin music, especially that played by the virtuosi, because everyone knows it is difficult to achieve and it affords proof of the player's technical attainments. But what are four notes compared to eighty-eight? Of course the piano is perfectly willing to sound the eighty-eight at once, but it is a little difficult for the performer who has only ten fingers to use. Some modern composers have suggested that the forearm may be used to strike a batch of adjacent notes, and so it can if you care for such an effect. Still even with ten notes at a time we are provided with a great many sounds, as many as ten wind instruments can make. We discover therefore that the piano is very valuable to provide harmony to accompany melodies. This easily makes it the most useful of instruments. We have been accustomed during the last seven hundred years to the agreeable sound of harmony. We like our melodies accompanied. Therefore the piano, which can both play a melody and accompany it at the same time, is the most independent instrument and the most self-sufficient. Also it can reproduce somewhat the effect of an orchestra or miscellaneous group of instruments. We have seen that in such reproduction, which is called *transcription,* the change of instrumentation to one not originally intended by the composer is inaccurate. It cannot give us the composer's exact music because in his original plan he took into account the properties of the instrument or instruments for which he was writing. This point will be worth reconsidering in a few paragraphs.

Let us compare the piano and the organ in number of notes that can be played simultaneously, a matter so necessary to the presentation of harmony. For the piano we have only ten fingers, for the organ we have ten fingers and two feet. With each foot we can sound two notes upon a specially designed foot keyboard. The heel can depress one note and the toe another provided that they are close enough together. Why is it necessary and why is the organist not contented with his ten fingers like the pianist? This question brings us to the *damper pedal* on the piano. This pedal, the one on the right, often referred to incorrectly as the "loud pedal," is very useful. In the first place by raising all the felts which dampen the strings it allows all sorts of stray harmonics to cause sympathetic vibrations on strings which have not been struck. This gives a rich sound to the tone. Try striking a single note on the keyboard with and again without the use of the damper pedal. You will see how much more mellow the tone is when you have employed it. Now the tone of the piano string, moribund although it is, is by no means without some survival value. With the damper pedal in use we can strike some low notes and then pass quickly up the keyboard so that many notes are all sounding together. The number of notes which can be caused to sound together depends upon the agility of our fingers. If we want to sound a chord, instead of sounding four notes and holding them as we should have to do on four wind instruments, we can strike them in succession. This sounding of the notes of a chord in succession is called an *arpeggio,* and is the particular property of the piano and the harp. The term is derived from the Italian word for harp, *arpa.* An arpeggio may be played upon any other instrument but the notes will not continue to sound together. Each sound stops as the next is reached. On the piano however there is no use holding down the note after it is struck. The damper pedal will continue the sound just as will the presence of the finger upon the key. We cannot keep the strings vibrating for a long time but we can set a great many of them in motion practically simultaneously with ten agile fingers. This great asset of the piano makes it possible to spread out the music over a large tonal area, and gain the exquisite effects found in such composers as Chopin and Liszt.

The organ, like other wind instruments, has no damper pedal. Its wonderful tone survival value depends upon keeping each note depressed as long as you want it to sound. An arpeggio on the organ doesn't give so much the effect of a simultaneous chord as it does on the piano. The result is that we cannot leave our keys and entrust the sounds to any helpful device. If we want the sounds to persist, we have to use up a finger. Ten fingers turn out to be entirely insufficient. If the right hand is playing the melody and the left the bass, there is a large gap of filling in harmony lacking. The result is that we use the feet to play the bass notes and fill in with the left hand. This gives the organ a wide tonal register to compare with the piano. But it is easy to see that the music will be of an entirely different sort. The organ music will be full of sustained slowly moving harmonies which would die out too quickly upon the piano, the piano music will move more rapidly and more often in the figures used to accompany melodies.

All these technical matters are too numerous for the listener to remember and must be a great strain upon the memory of the composer. How does he know all about these instruments and how can he write for them without being able to play them? The answer is that traditions of the use and the properties of instruments are so well established that much of our knowledge of them is instinctive. When a composer writes a piece for organ he has undoubtedly heard enough organ music so that he unconsciously imitates the best methods of writing for the instrument. Without realizing it, we become familiar with the habits and preferences of the instruments. What we know as the standard symphony orchestra is an ensemble which represents the growth of much painful experimentation on the part of seventeenth- and eighteenth-century composers. What instruments would sound well together, how to employ each so that it would contribute to the whole and not stand out when submergence was to be desired, all these subtleties of arrangement were discovered for us by the musicians of yesterday. We find the results recorded in the works of the composers. If we begin by imitating the works of these men, we learn gradually a mass of fact and detail that would be impossible to assimilate if undertaken fact by fact and instrument by instrument. This is the way that the composer learns to write for orchestra. The listener may follow him at a respectful distance, acquiring knowledge instinctively by listening to good works, but never missing an opportunity, if some particular instrumental effect pleases or displeases him greatly, of asking why.

Tradition has given us the symphony orchestra of four choirs, woodwinds, brass, percussion and strings. The expressive possibilities of this arrangement of instruments are enormous and far from being exhausted as yet. We have the military band, composed entirely of wind instruments and percussion. The reason why the band uses no strings is that it is designed to play in the open air and the tone of strings loses its carrying quality when taken outdoors. In a band arrangement, the clarinets replace the violins as the main melodic instruments of the ensemble. *Chamber music* is played by an ensemble of instruments designed to sound well in a small room. Here we find the string quartet, one or more instruments combined with piano, small groups of wind instruments, voice and accompaniment, and various ensembles which are prepared to emphasize subtlety of detail rather than prodigiousness of effect. This is the most sensi-

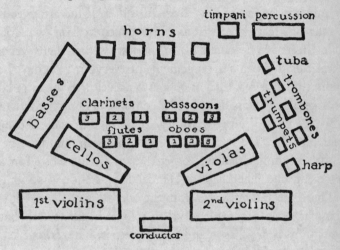

STANDARD SEATING PLAN OF SYMPHONY ORCHESTRA

tive sort of music, not so popular with the large public but perhaps the most enduring joy to every lover of the art. We speak of *salon music* in contradistinction to chamber music in that its purpose is often more social than purely musical. Where social values are paramount, music is never taken quite so seriously. The guests must be entertained, the music must not be too serious in nature and the performance is preferably somewhat showy. In the case of chamber music, the audience is expected to listen and submerge its ego in the presence of great examples of the art.

Transcription was spoken of a few pages back. The most familiar kind of transcriptions are orchestral and opera pieces arranged for the piano or organ. The transcription of a symphony may serve an excellent purpose in familiarizing a wider public with the work, but as we have seen the sound is only approximate and values will suffer. If the arranger is a man of great skill in transcription, such as Liszt, remarkable effects can be obtained. In the last century there was a great rage for piano arrangements of everything. Today the transcription is regarded as on a lower level than the original arrangement unless done by the composer himself or a man of equal gifts. We prefer to hear our music as imagined by the composer, and with reason. Many transcriptions have become so familiar that we forget they originally existed in a different state. The *Largo* of Handel, for instance, was a song for baritone and orchestra from the opera *Xerxes*. Today it is familiar as an organ piece, violin solo, even piano solo, but we rarely hear it as Handel intended it. The *Hungarian Rhapsodies* of Liszt were written for piano, not orchestra; and the piano music of Bach was conceived for two entirely different types of instrument, the clavichord and harpsichord, both of which are now rarely played.

There is an interesting point to be observed about music designed for the harpsichord. This instrument preceded the piano, which did not come into general use until the end of the eighteenth century. All the music of Bach, Handel, Rameau, Couperin and Scarlatti, which we hear played on the piano, was mostly intended for the harpsichord, a plucking, not a percussion instrument. As the key on the harpsichord is depressed, a jack comes up and plucks the string.

There is no accent possible because no matter how vigorously the key is struck, the volume of tone is constant. Several sets of jacks were sometimes used to vary the tone color as the different stops do on the organ. This gave the instrument a resource which the piano does not have, but on the other hand there was no damper pedal to keep the strings sounding. The problem of playing harmony on the harpsichord was somewhat like that of the organ. The harpsichordist did not use his feet to cover additional territory but he did have couplers which he could draw to double the note on the octave above or below. These made it possible to play twenty or even forty notes with his ten fingers.

Let us examine a piece of harpsichord music of the eighteenth century. The first thing we notice is that the melody is ornamented with many trills and turns. These were not put there merely for ornamental purposes but to serve as accents. Each turn calls our attention to one note as distinct from its companions. On the piano these ornamented accents are superfluous; we have much simpler means at our disposal. Notice also that a short phrase of a few measures very often repeats itself literally in a way which sounds rather dull on the piano. On the harpsichord the effect was varied by using a different set of jacks so that it seemed almost as if one instrument were echoing the music of another. Sometimes, too, the music sounds thin when we play it on the piano. In many passages the harpsichordist was using his octave couplers, so that the music was practically doubled in extent. Musicians who arrange harpsichord music for the piano often take these considerations into account, suppress some of the excessive ornamentation and repeats and add octaves in the thin

places. This gives a much better approximation of the effect
that the eighteenth-century composer intended.

Instrumentation, the study of the potentialities and preferences of the different instruments, is a fascinating subject. In
general the more we know about them the more we shall enjoy music. When an instrument has been treated with such
understanding as Palestrina has treated the voice, Chopin the
piano, Paganini the violin, Wagner the orchestra, Sousa the
band and Bach the organ, we are delighted. Sometimes it
sounds so well that we forget to notice that the actual content
of the music may be less good. A Beethoven sonata, for instance, may sound less well on the piano than a piece of Liszt,
but it is usually infinitely better music. There are many composers who have the genius of arrangement less well developed than others but whose music we may prefer. Although
the choral music of Bach may be less well conceived for the
voice than Handel's, we may still like it better because we
find its content richer.

Some music we strongly suspect is written for show. Audiences like to witness performers who can play obviously difficult music. This feeling is somewhat akin to the wonder we
experience in watching an expert trapeze artist or juggler; it
is a treat for the eye, not for the ear, which has much simpler
tastes in music. We should not be too stern in denying audiences this pleasure. Let anyone enjoy the art in any way he
cares to. The only point to be observed is that the eye will
cheat the ear out of its pleasure if it can. The eye doesn't care
for the sound of the music at all, all it wants is the fun of
watching very rapid and expert movements. Meanwhile the
ear is not working at all. The music may be good, bad or in-

different, the ear alone can tell. Virtuoso effects sometimes are a positive handicap to the logical development of the musical ideas. We must not forget that the instruments exist as a medium for musical ideas, not to show themselves off. Let us leave them and turn our attention to music itself.

CHAPTER IV

Rhythm

MUSIC consists of a succession of tones, presented one at a time or in combination. In either case we observe that they are governed by definite time relationships. This is naturally to be expected because in all forms of art we must have organization into patterns which the mind can assimilate and understand. The shapes which we find in architecture, painting, and sculpture are space patterns; those employed in poetry and music are time patterns. Poetry and music are known therefore as time arts. In order to understand a time art our memories must assist us, because details are presented singly, and the work can only exist as a whole in our minds. In the consideration of space arts we see the ensemble of details first and can examine each detail in relation to the whole without the effort of memory or mental re-creation.

In a time art such as music, the time relationships must be sufficiently simple and definite for the mind to comprehend them. The organization of music in time is called *rhythm*. It is easy to prove by experimentation that sounds without such organization make no lasting impression upon our consciousness. On the other hand this rhythmic organization is so much a part of our conception of music that even divorced from the tones which it employs, a melody may be identified by its rhythm alone.

Try the experiment of tapping or clapping the rhythm of a familiar tune like *Dixie* or *The Star Spangled Banner*. You will discover that not only can it be identified at once, but your mind will supply the missing tones. If you reverse the experiment and sing the tones without the rhythm you will find that the tune is much harder to identify.

Much of the color and personality of music proceeds from its rhythm. This may be slow or fast, even or uneven, with accents frequent or infrequent. Combination of these elements give rhythm its character. The emotional effect of music depends largely upon the type of rhythm which it employs. For example it is easy to improvise or imagine rhythms which could be identified as martial, funereal, swinging, solemn, barbaric, or jazz. It will be observed that all rhythms consist of accents or the alternation of accented and unaccented beats. When these accents occur frequently, the music is stirring; when they occur at long intervals, a tranquil effect is obtained. When they occur with too great similarity, the music becomes monotonous. The unexpected accent brings an element of surprise which gives life to the music. If they occur without apparent plan, the effect is chaotic.

We shall discover, then, that there must be a degree of periodicity to the appearance of accents in a rhythm if the mind is to grasp it, but that variety within a predictable plan is desirable and even necessary.

It is possible to show by experiment that rhythms may be combined. The mind can understand two rhythms heard simultaneously if proper relationships are established. Try, by tapping, the combination of a simple recurring rhythm with one which is faster and more irregular. You will see that such combination is an agreeable one and not difficult to establish.

The demand for periodic recurrence in a rhythm is so great, however, that practically all rhythmic organization is based upon one of two general schemes, strong alternating with a weak beat, or strong followed by two weak beats. The first type is known as *binary,* the second as *ternary* rhythm. One or the other of these types is found to underlie the rhythmic framework of every composition. For example, *Old Black Joe* and *Dixie* are binary; *America* and *The Star Spangled Banner* are ternary. The typical rhythm of the march is binary and that of the waltz is ternary. The student should examine a number of familiar and unfamiliar melodies until this difference is easily distinguishable. It is helpful to beat time when listening to a melody because the body instinctively adjusts itself to these rhythms and assists in their identification.

The underlying binary or ternary rhythm of two or three beats is known as the *fundamental rhythm*. Sub-divisions of these beats which appear within the general framework are called the *subsidiary rhythm*. You will observe this distinction if you watch a conductor. He does not make a motion of the baton for every note. If he did the forces under his control would be soon dissipated and the general plan of the rhythm would not be felt by the performers. He indicates the fundamental plan by his beat, and by adherence to this plan, order in performance is achieved.

The subsidiary rhythm is therefore the variation of accented and unaccented beats over the general plan of the fundamental scheme. This will be clear to you if you examine a simple rhythm like *Yankee Doodle*. This is based upon a beat of *two*. In each case the accent corresponds with the natural way that you would beat *one*. There are subsidiary notes in this rhythm but they occur without much variation. Almost every beat of the fundamental rhythm allows for two of the subsidiary rhythm. Now compare this effect with an examination of the fundamental and subsidiary rhythm of *America*. This is ternary and the beat will be in *three*. Taking three beats as a group, notice that in the first six groups, the subsidiary rhythm is identical with the fundamental rhythm in first, third and fifth, but that in second, fourth and sixth there is variety. Continuing with the melody you will notice that toward the end there is even greater variety. This variety of subsidiary rhythm makes *America* a more interesting melody than *Yankee Doodle*. We find that in music where there is too great similarity between fundamental and subsidiary rhythm the effect is monotonous. A more elaborate scheme is found in Sousa's March, *The Stars and Stripes Forever*. You will notice that there is not a single rhythmic group in which the subsidiary rhythm is the same as the fundamental binary rhythm. Some of the beats of the fundamental rhythm are silent, with the subsidiary rhythm in repose. Again there are accents in the latter which occur on neither the strong nor the weak beat of the fundamental rhythm.

We call a fundamental rhythmic group a *measure* of the music, and it will be seen that a measure in music roughly corresponds to a foot in verse meter. There is a system of measurement employed in music which provides for the in-

dication of the fundamental rhythmic scheme of a composition, as well as the actual rhythm which includes the subsidiary rhythm. The following symbols are used to indicate
note values:

𝅝	WHOLE NOTE
𝅗𝅥	HALF NOTE
♩	QUARTER NOTE
♪	EIGHTH NOTE
𝅘𝅥𝅯	SIXTEENTH NOTE
𝅘𝅥𝅰	THIRTY-SECOND NOTE
𝅘𝅥𝅱	SIXTY-FOURTH NOTE

Any one of these note values may be taken as a unit of measure. If, for instance, we take the quarter note as unit of measure, binary rhythm will have two of these in a group or
measure, and ternary will have three. For variation of the
subsidiary rhythm, if we want four notes in a single measure
of duple rhythm, we shall use four eighth notes; if we want
only one, a half note is indicated. Therefore it will be seen
that the fundamental rhythmic scheme does not prescribe
that there shall be a note for every beat, but merely that
each measure correspond to the elapsed time value of the
number of beats indicated by the underlying binary or ternary
rhythm.

The metrical system also makes provision for the following
series of *rests* or silent beats:

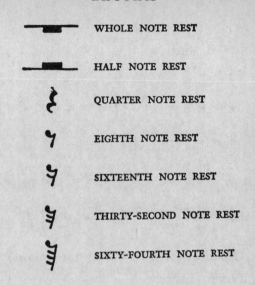

WHOLE NOTE REST

HALF NOTE REST

QUARTER NOTE REST

EIGHTH NOTE REST

SIXTEENTH NOTE REST

THIRTY-SECOND NOTE REST

SIXTY-FOURTH NOTE REST

Other devices are necessary to record uneven rhythms. For instance, if we wish three notes to have the value of one, we are somewhat embarrassed because our system provides only for halving values. We accordingly use three notes of half the indicated value, group them together, and place the figure three above them. This device is known as the *triplet*. If we wish to prolong a note for only half its value, a dot is placed after the note, or it is possible to add another note of half the value to the first and join them below or above by a semi-circle. This is known as the *tie*. It will be noticed that *bar-lines* serve as an indication of the metrical divisions.

With these symbols at our disposal, let us note exactly the rhythms of *America,* which is triple, and *Old Black Joe,* which is duple.

AMERICA

♩ UNIT OF MEASURE

OLD BLACK JOE (*Omitting the Chorus*)

♩ UNIT OF MEASURE

The meter of a composition is indicated at the beginning by a *time-signature*. This is a fraction expressed in this fashion, 2/4, 3/4, 2/2, or 3/8. The figure below stands for the unit of measure; the figure above tells how many of these or their equivalent are to be included in a metrical division, the *bar*, or the space between bar-lines.

Meter may be simple or compound. A bar may consist of a single measure of rhythm, or it may consist of two, three, or four. *Simple meter,* which is called for by the signatures in the last paragraph, has one measure to a bar, but the signatures 4/4, 6/8, 9/8, etc., call for *compound meter* which includes more than one measure in a bar. Traditionally there is only one strong accent in a bar. This comes directly after the bar-line. The inclusion of two or more measures in a single bar weakens the accents of all but the first group. A melody with fewer accents of the rhythm may therefore be more accurately expressed in a compound meter.

The meter 4/4 calls for alternate strong and weak accents. We find it often used for lyric melodies in binary rhythm. An example of this is *Loch Lomond.* The effect of this melody as it would sound if written with 2/4 meter would be quite different. Try it and notice that there will be too many accents for the character of the melody. Remember that the meter is only an arbitrary framework for the recording of the fundamental rhythm. It provides a convenient pattern of accents. The composer chooses the meter which best suits the rhythm he has in mind.

6/8 meter is often confusing to the student because it consists of two measures of triple rhythm in a bar of the meter. In this case the rhythm is triple but the meter is duple. A melody in 6/8 meter may sound like 3/4, because the rhythmic groupings into threes will be immediately apparent. However there is a swing to 6/8 meter due to the alternation of accents in each bar, whereas in 3/4 the strong accents come regularly in succession. Good examples of 6/8 meter are to be found in the folk songs *Believe Me If All Those Endearing*

Young Charms and *Bonnie Dundee*. 9/8 provides for three measures of triple rhythm in a bar and 12/8 for four. 6/4 is an interesting metrical signature because it may consist of three measures of duple rhythm, or two of three. Brahms uses this signature frequently, and combines the two rhythmic possibilities simultaneously in melody and accompaniment.

The signatures 5/4 and 7/4, etc., give to the music an irregular effect because they combine in a single bar units of both duple and triple rhythm. In 5/4 meter, which is the most frequently employed, a regular plan is usually followed of a succession of two beats plus three, or three beats plus two.

It will be seen from the above that meter and rhythm are not the same thing. Much confusion exists in the use of these terms, as well as the terms bar and measure. For our purposes let us regard meter as the device used to record and support the great rhythmic framework which includes all the time organization of the composition. Let us call metrical divisions bars rather than measures. They are often identical, especially in the case of simple meter, but as we have seen they do not agree at all in compound meter.

If we return to a consideration of the conductor's beat, we shall see that he indicates by his beats the metrical framework of the composition. There is always a down beat for the first count of the bar. In the case of 2/4, his baton moves down-up, for 3/4 down-right-up, for 4/4 down-left-right-up. In the case of 6/8 meter if the time is slow he indicates all six beats, but for fast 6/8 time, he only indicates the two rhythmic groups, and his baton moves down-up.

It is a good idea to learn to beat time according to musical tradition. Not only is it a useful accomplishment which you may find helpful in leading informal music, but it helps to identify and understand rhythms. You have probably observed that college song leaders at football games very seldom give a clear indication of the metrical beat. If the music is familiar, this does not particularly matter, but let one of them try to conduct an unfamiliar composition by the combination of dancing and acrobatics which they employ, and the result is an unhappy one. Compare the song leader's methods with the conductor of the college band. His behavior is less spectacular but it keeps the music together.

We have seen that rhythm is almost always based upon a fundamental scheme which can be easily grasped. There is another feature about it which is characteristic and inevitable. It must provide for occasional moments of repose. If you examine the rhythm of any piece of music you will discover that these reposes occur periodically and often. Without them the strain of listening to an extended piece would be unendurable. The periodic repose which occurs in a rhythmic scheme is called *cadence*. The cadence divides the rhythm into *rhythmic phrases*. As the measure of rhythm corresponds to the foot in verse, a rhythmic phrase corresponds to a line of verse.

In verse we have names for lines of varying length such as hexameter, pentameter, etc., but there is nothing in the metrical system which indicates the phrase length of the rhythm. Generally speaking, however, you will find rhythmic phrases are presented in groups of four. That is, after four or eight bars of the music you will instinctively expect and will usually get a rhythmic cadence. In the simple folk song there are generally only four phrases. Experiment with any of the simple melodies which we have examined and see if you can pick out the division into phrases. You will note that *America* consists of two phrases, the first one six bars in length and the second eight. The majority of the others, however, will naturally divide into four phrases of four bars each.

This last pattern is such a familiar one that we are surprised when simple melodies deviate from it. Examine the

BALLAD OF THE SINFUL RICH MAN

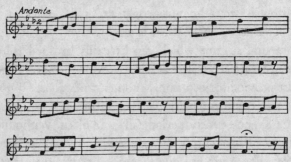

French folk tune, *Ballad of the Sinful Rich Man*. You will find the division into phrases quite irregular. The first phrase consists of six bars, the second six, the third four, and the fourth three. Do you like the effect of this irregularity or does it disturb you? In any event it makes the melody a little more difficult to grasp.

You will find that even the most elaborate music, no matter how long, may easily be divided into its constituent phrases, and that grouping by four is the usual rule. One reason why the music of Brahms is often baffling at first hearing is that he uses irregular phrase lengths very often. When you have become accustomed to his rhythmic personality, you may come to regard this feature of his music as an asset. On the other hand you may always prefer music which is more regularly divided.

Understanding of the rhythmic phrase is so important in grasping unfamiliar music at a single hearing that it will be worth our while to study some actual details which can be discovered upon examination. Listening for these details, which are not tremendously important in themselves, provides concrete exercises which help to develop sustained attention.

The first of these concerns itself with phrase beginnings. Sometimes we find an accent at the very beginning of the phrase, sometimes there are several unaccented notes which precede the first accent. The latter feature is called *anacrusis* (Greek—*to strike up*). Examples of anacrusis are found in the first phrase of *The Star Spangled Banner, My Old Kentucky Home* and *Dixie*. To conduct them, therefore, we shall have to start with an up beat so that the down beat parallels the first accent. *Old Black Joe* and *America* start with the first accent and have no anacrusis in the first phrase.

The other feature is the matter of accent in the phrase ending. If the phrase ends with an accented note, we call it a *masculine ending*. If there are unaccented notes to conclude, it is a *feminine ending*. The former is much more common and stronger in effect, but the latter gives subtlety and smoothness to the succession of phrases. For instance in *Old Black Joe* the phrase endings are all masculine, but the first phrase ending in *Carry Me Back to Old Virginny* is feminine because the last accent comes before the last note.

An examination of the separate phrases of folk songs will

show you that, in a given song, they tend to repeat each other. Sometimes the rhythm is repeated and the melody slightly changed; often they are identical. This is another characteristic of rhythmic organization which is an aid to our perception, because only by repetition can the time art imprint itself clearly upon the consciousness. The second time you hear a phrase you understand it better, and there is much

THE LONDONDERRY AIR

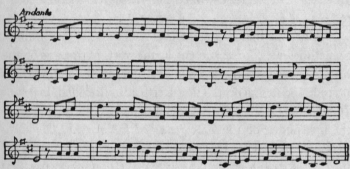

pleasure in recognizing something which you have heard before.

The first two phrases of *The Star Spangled Banner* are exactly alike; in *Old Black Joe* the rhythm of the first three is identical. In *Drink To Me Only With Thine Eyes* and *All Through The Night* the first, second and fourth phrases are identical. The lovely *Londonderry Air* has the same rhythm for all four phrases but a different melody for the third and fourth.

Another characteristic of the rhythmic phrase is that there are often rhythmic groupings which repeat themselves in the same phrase. Such a grouping we call a *rhythmic idea*. It gives its personality to the entire song. *The Volga Boat Song,* for instance, begins in the first bar with a rhythmic idea which is repeated twice in the same phrase and is similarly treated in the last phrase. The first two bars of *America* consist of a rhythmic idea which is several times repeated in the two phrases of the song, although it does not always appear with the original notes.

These features of the rhythmic phrase are not confined to folk songs. You will see that they are often in evidence when you proceed to the analysis of large instrumental and choral works, and that they give unity and clarity to the rhythmic design.

We have spoken of a fast or slow rhythm. The effect of a rhythm certainly depends upon the speed with which it is performed. This speed does not affect the internal organization of the rhythm but is an important factor in its personality. We call the relative motion of rhythm its *tempo.* This is indicated at the beginning of the composition, generally by the use of an Italian term. The principal tempo indications are *lento, adagio, andante, allegretto, allegro,* and *presto,* ranging from very slow to very fast. These instructions are occasionally modified by a descriptive term such as *poco,* a little, *con moto,* with spirit, *tranquillo,* smoothly, *con brio,* with brilliance, etc. In a long work different tempo indications may be used for various sections. We also have terms to indicate slowing up the rhythm, *ritardando,* and increasing its pace, *accelerando.*

In the time of Beethoven an instrument was invented to give greater precision to tempo indications—the *metronome.* By means of a metronome mark the composer may indicate how many notes of a certain value he wishes to be executed in a minute. At the beginning of compositions since Beethoven you will often find a metronomic direction indicated in this fashion, $\quad \downarrow = 40$.

Pronounced irregularity within an established tempo is called *rubato*. It is an expressive device somewhat corresponding to vibrato or portamento in tone, useful but capable of abuse. You will notice that the Strauss Waltzes are usually played with rubato effect, certain phrases dwelt upon and certain others quickened perceptibly. This eliminates the monotony that would result in a too strict adherence to the tempo of the simple waltz. Chopin is said to have played with a discreet rubato which resembled the swaying of the branches of a tree. Certain temperamental pianists play his music as if the branches were no longer attached to a trunk. There is no doubt that performers and conductors often distort the sense of the rhythm by a too liberal use of the device.

We have seen that the metrical system calls for regular accents, the strongest of which occurs immediately after the bar. Rhythms, on the other hand, seldom demand such regularity of accent, although the underlying beat of two or three is the basis of their organization. For this reason performers must take the unimaginative accents of the metrical system with a grain of salt. Not all first accents should be equally strong; the rhythmic flow and organization must be taken into account if a musical effect is to be achieved. In a musical phrase there are usually one or two outstanding accents. They may occur on a normally unaccented beat of the meter, or even between beats as in the case of the *Stars and Stripes Forever*. The strong accentuation of a weak or silent beat is called *syncopation*. This device is the usual basis for jazz music but is by no means peculiar to it. The chief difference between the syncopations of the masters of the symphony and the celebrities of jazz is that in the case of the latter they occur more frequently and more regularly, so that they become the principal feature of the music.

There is no way of indicating that the first beat of a meter is not to be given a strong accent. That is left to the musicianship and rhythmic understanding of the performer. Irregular accents may be called for by the sign, >, over the note, or the letters *sf,* abbreviation of the Italian term, *sforzando,* written under the note.

Rhythm in music has a twofold origin. Its most obvious source is in the primitive dance. Bodily gestures tend to great regularity of movement. In earliest times, the dance was confined to the two principal occupations of the savage, war and lovemaking, both involving the emotions. Although as civilization progressed, refinement of impulse was produced in the dance, the original primitive suggestion is to be found lurking behind most dance-inspired music. Our bodies are very suggestible to the rhythms of gesture. When such rhythms are produced, we are actually stimulated physically, enjoying vicariously the movement which we hear portrayed. We shall therefore discover that much of the emotional appeal of music comes from the rhythm of the dance.

The other source of rhythm is the one which it shares with speech. The expressive cries of the savage, which turned into language, also found their expression in song. Song is really language emotionalized by tone into melody. The kind of musical rhythm which proceeds from speech will naturally be more subtle than the other; for bodily gesture, refined or unrefined, can scarcely compete with language for range and accuracy of expression.

The history of music shows us the interplay of these two elements of rhythm. In the Middle Ages and before that time, choral music was cultivated to a much greater extent than instrumental music. Instruments were in use but not in a highly developed state. In the music of the early Christian Church, rhythms are very elaborate and un-dancelike, for they are primarily under the influence of words. Instruments were chiefly used to accompany the dance. When opera came to the fore at the beginning of the seventeenth century, the elements of song and dance were united; choral music borrowed from the rhythms of the dance, and instrumental music began to borrow from the song. As a result we have instrumental music which is so subtle and intellectual in its rhythmic content that it must have proceeded from word rhythm. On the other hand, our popular songs are often so primitive in effect that they are really dances, not songs.

In the music of today, which includes everything which has been written in this century, we find some very complicated effects. Some modern rhythms are impossible to note without frequent change of time signature. Sometimes composers change the time signature when a simpler means of notation might be used. The experiment has been made of omitting all time signature, as in Gregorian chant. When a bar appears an accent follows, but the values within the bar are all determined by the relative length of the note symbols used. With this sort of notation, performers experience the same difficulty which in the Middle Ages produced the metrical system. And so our art continues to move in cycles. It must be said, however, that there are many fresh rhythmical effects yet to be achieved within the limits of our traditional metrical system, provided it is sufficiently understood by the composer.

CHAPTER V

Melody

MELODY is such a familiar part of music that to define it seems hardly necessary. When we do the result is not entirely satisfactory, because exact definition imposes limitations upon a term rich in subjective meaning. Strictly speaking, it is a succession of sounds with rhythmic and tonal organization. In popular interpretation it is used almost as a term of endearment meaning musical essence. We speak of the *melody* of verse when we may mean *rhythm,* of *melodiousness* of sound when *harmony* would be more exact. In the study of the elements of music we must, however, limit the term to an objective meaning as represented by the above definition.

There are probably many questions which the reader will want to ask about melody: what makes it memorable, what is the difference between a melody and a tune, how is a melody organized, what makes it beautiful, why one melody is better than another, and why some compositions seem to be entirely without it. Some of these questions are easier to answer than others. The most important help toward remembering a melody is familiarity. The melodies which you particularly like are usually the familiar ones. You probably cannot recall the first time you ever heard such popular melodies as *Loch Lomond* or *Annie Laurie;* you may have heard them many times before you were aware of them at all. After they became sufficiently familiar to overcome the natural inertia of your ear, you began to be conscious of their beauty and to remember them. Perhaps you can recall pieces which you didn't like at all at first, but later became favorites. Theodore Thomas once said: "Popular music is familiar music."

Merchants who specialize in selling music to the public realize this truth. They can create popularity by bombarding your ears with their tunes. This is done in musical comedies when one tune is selected for repetition during the performance until even the dullest ears have captured it. Music publishers plan great radio, restaurant and dance orchestra campaigns for their new works. It is rumored that the popularity of the *Maine Stein Song,* which you may recall with sorrow, was an experiment to see just how effective such campaigns could be when undertaken on behalf of a song of proved mediocrity. You know the result.

You may say, "Well, I don't like the *Maine Stein Song.* I am tired of it." This perfectly natural feeling brings us to the observation that melodies may lose a certain amount of charm when they become too familiar. There seems to be a point of saturation beyond which applications of a melody to the ear are less effective. It will not be hard to understand that the better the melody, the longer deferred this point of saturation; also that in some instances the process of familiarization may be slower. Some melodies are so good that we never tire of them. Some very good melodies contain sufficient repetition to impress our ears more quickly than others. Others may be so subtle that we can never come to like them. Our tastes vary enormously, as do the melodic gifts of even the greatest composers. Some melodies seem so absolutely inspired, so simple and fresh, that we admit them at once to the category of tunes and cherish them indefinitely.

Just what is the difference between a melody and a tune? The dictionary does not distinguish between them particularly. Are they the same thing? Perhaps you have sung hymns in church. Hymns are certainly familiar tunes. While you were singing the tune, a large man near you may have begun singing the bass or your aunt with a rich spiritual nature chimed in with the alto. What were they singing if not the tune? Or suppose you were listening to a familiar orchestra piece like the *Unfinished Symphony* of Schubert. There were certainly tunes easy to recognize in the strings or the winds, but what were the other instruments playing? Now anything which is singable is certainly a melody; so the alto and bass of the hymns, while not tunes, were authentic melodies. Also in a symphony there are apparently subsidiary melodies in addition to the tunes.

A tune, then, is a melody which is familiar enough for us to recognize, standing out from any other melodies which may accompany it. It is really a subjective classification for melodies which we have made our own. But if we insist upon tunes alone, we shall be depriving much other melody of the right to exist. By definition the term *melody* includes any organized succession of musical tones.

We have examined some of the laws of rhythmical and tonal organization. It is from these elements that melody is created. Why not make the definition still broader, attributing the term melody to any succession of sounds? Do we need this organization? Why isn't the howl of the savage a melody? We can appreciate a continuous curve in a line; we do not insist that this curve be a series of recognizable points like our system of tones. Helmholtz, who gave us the theory of tone character, has an interesting answer to this. He says that a line exists in space so that the eye may see the whole and examine it backwards and forwards at leisure. In melody, however, we progress from one tone to another, with no opportunity of surveying the whole at once. In order to grasp the logic of this movement, we must understand where we are at each instant.

We shall first examine the rhythmic features of melodic progression and then turn our attention to the laws governing the succession of tones. We have already noticed the close relation existing between rhythm and melody. When we come to separate the two elements we find that it is easier to state a rhythm without its accompanying melody than it is to isolate the melody from the rhythm. We found that we could recognize a tune from its rhythm alone. The tonal succession without the rhythm is almost entirely lacking in individuality. Because it is so much under the domination of its accompanying element, melody easily adjusts itself to the divisions of phrase called for by the rhythm; a melodic phrase corresponds exactly to a phrase of the rhythm.

To the musical characteristics of the phrase given by rhythm, primary rhythm, subsidiary rhythm, accent, grouping by measures and tempo, melody adds an important contribution, *cadence*. Cadence in music serves the same purpose as cadence in speech. The sentence in prose corresponds to the line of verse or the phrase of music. Division into sentences is marked by cadence or fall of the voice. These cadences are not all precisely similar. At the end of the paragraph or a particularly important sentence the fall is perhaps greater. We have lesser divisions represented by the comma, the semicolon and the reverse of the cadence where the voice by rising asks a question and because it is suspended seems to demand further speech as if in answer. You will notice in the speech of even the most unskilled speakers great variety of cadence. It adds much to the intelligibility of the thought expressed.

In melody, cadence adds to rhythmic organization in division of phrase. As in speech, we have a great variety of cadence. Some of this is contributed by the harmony or accompanying sounds, but melodies seem to have this feature even when unaccompanied. Let us examine the phrase endings of some familiar songs and see if we can discover any general principles.

Sing or play the melodies we have already studied, such as *Yankee Doodle* and *Old Black Joe* starting on C. Now try *Believe Me If All Those Endearing Young Charms* starting on E. Do you notice that each of the songs ends on C with a final cadence which is unmistakable? Not only the two songs which start on C but the one which began on E seem to regard C as their most important note, the one which they must reach in order to give a sense of completion. That is because all the three melodies are based upon the scale of C, using the familiar Greek tones in melodic and rhythmic succession. This scale of C has for its fundamental note or *tonic* the tone C, and this tone is so important that we seem to require it for final or *full cadence*. You will notice from *Believe Me* that we need not start upon the tonic.

Now notice the end of the first and second phrases of *Old Black Joe*. There is undoubtedly a feeling of cadence due to the rhythm. How about the melody? The first phrase ends on G, the second on D. We call them *suspensive* cadences because they are not *conclusive* as the full cadence on C. They seem to make us want to go on, although they permit us to pause. Sometimes we have a conclusive cadence in the middle of a song. There is one in *America*. There certainly seems less incentive to go on after the word "sing" than there is in each phrase of *Old Black Joe*. You will notice that melodies which reserve the conclusive cadence for the final phrase have a greater sense of continuity than those in which it appears prematurely.

To return to the suspensive cadences on G and D, do you find one less suspensive than the other? Could you conceivably stop on the D and make sense? How about the G? If we had to break off at that point, wouldn't it be less outrageous to our musical feelings? Why should this be?

Before answering the question let us seek some more data. Notice the melodic phrase endings in *Believe Me*. They are successively E, C, E, and C. The first cadence on C gives the effect of an ending; we notice that the whole melodic phrase is exactly like the final one. Since the ending must be conclusive and this phrase wishes to be exactly like the ending, it too will have to be conclusive. How about the ending on E? Is this as suspensive as the D in *Old Black Joe*? If this comparison is too difficult for you, try some alterations of the ending of the first phrase of *Believe Me*. The next to the last note is D. Play for an ending of the phrase two Ds instead of D, E. Do you notice that the E is less suspensive than the D? Now since you have begun maltreating *Believe Me,* why not compile some statistics about the use of the various notes of the scale as phrase endings? Substitute for the original ending of this phrase every note of the scale in turn. Only the octave will prove to be conclusive and this because it is a duplication of the tonic or fundamental. Of the rest, two notes will be less suspensive than the others, the E and the G.

There is a natural explanation of this cadence feeling of E and G in the key of C which we can find if we again consider the system of harmonics or partial tones. We found that the first four overtones of the tone of C are as follows, C (the octave above), G, C (two octaves above the fundamental) and E. These tones, therefore, are very closely related to the tonic and naturally share somewhat in its cadence feeling. The other tones of the scale of C either lie outside the system of overtones or appear too remotely to make them share in this feeling.

The study of cadence has brought us unsuspectingly into a consideration of the laws governing the succession of tones in a melody. We learned from the chapter on tone that music is made from a selected series of tones which we inherited from the Greeks. These tones have been arranged by custom into familiar scales, the most common of which is represented by our C major scale. The scale is somewhat analogous to an alphabet; from its constituent notes or *degrees,* melodies may be formed as words from the alphabet. By limiting our melodies to a known scale, we conform to the principle stated by

Helmholtz, that we must understand the relationship of each tone to every other in order to comprehend melodic progression. Familiarity with the sound of the scale, so that we can recognize each degree if we know the tonic as a point of departure, will help us to appreciate the logic and beauty of a given melody. We shall discover upon closer acquaintance with the scale that each degree has its own individuality and melodic tendency. We have already discovered that the third and the fifth degree have somewhat of the cadence feeling of the tonic, but that this is lacking in the other notes of the scale. By experiment, you may perhaps discover that in a melody the seventh degree tends to rise whereas the fourth tends slightly downward. In skipping from one note to another, large leaps are necessarily less natural than small ones, but the most awkward skip of all, one which all singers detest, is the skip from the fourth to the seventh degree. This is called the skip of the *tritone* because the notes are separated by three full tones. Because of its awkwardness, we seldom find the skip of the tritone in a melody. Composers will go to the extent of raising the fourth or lowering the seventh degree by a half tone (thus using F sharp or B flat which are not in the scale) to avoid it.

We have seen that we can reproduce our C major scale pattern on any note on the piano providing we adjust by the black notes the arrangement of whole and half steps. When we do this and use different tones, although using the same scale pattern, we say that we are in a different key. We take the name of our key from the note on which we start, and in the *key signature* we show what white notes are to be raised by sharps or lowered bv flats. No matter what key we are in, the sound of the scale is the same and its notes will have the same relationship, the first one constituting the tonic.

It would seem then that we use only one scale in our modern melodies; that is, melodies since the time of Bach. Is this true? Let us experiment.

Can you remember the first part of the melody of Chopin's *Funeral March?* Here is the rhythmic scheme of the first four phrases.

Notice that the rhythm of the first, second and fourth phrases is the same and that of the third is varied. Try playing these four short phrases on the piano starting on C. Something is wrong. The fifth note cannot be found among any of the white notes. Also in the third phrase the second and third notes of the first measure give us difficulty. Suppose you try again and start on A. This seems to fit, doesn't it? These four phrases are all selected from a scale of seven notes starting on A. This is a different scale from our usual one made up of white notes in the key of C. We call it the *minor mode*. When we speak of a composition being in minor, we mean that the melody is based upon this scale. It resembles the old *Aeolian mode*. The other scale which we call the major is a duplication of the old *Ionian mode*.

The minor scale is not entirely independent. It is so much influenced by the major scale that we speak of each minor key as *relative* to some major, the one specifically which has the same key signature. The relative minor scale uses the same tones as its related major but starts on a tonic to be found three degrees below the major tonic (counting this as one). Therefore the relative minor of C is A.

Now examine the constitution of this minor scale. We find the first half step coming between the second and third degree instead of the third and fourth as in the case of the major. This gives the effect of a lowered third which is the distinguishing characteristic of the minor mode and is supposed to give it its melancholy character.

Play up the scale of C lowering the third by using E flat instead of E, but use all white notes for the rest of it. Does that sound right? It seems quite satisfactory, doesn't it? Now try the third phrase of the *Funeral March* again. It doesn't work much better than before. The sixth and seventh degrees of the scale are wrong. Then why did the scale sound right when we played it? The answer brings us to a curious tradition about the minor mode. When we play it moving upwards it is just like the major with the exception of the lowered third. When we play down we play its proper tones, the ones which are to be found on the white notes beginning with A. If we play the minor scale upwards beginning on C we use only E flat as a black note, but if we play down, we also use B flat and A flat to reproduce the proper arrangement of whole and half steps of the *true minor*. (C minor is relative to E flat

major, which has three flats.) If we play the minor scale up
from A we shall borrow F sharp and G sharp from the A
major scale. Going down we play the true minor which on
A uses only white notes. This curious tradition is due to the
fact that the major scale is so strong in its influence that
when our melodies ascend we actually borrow the sixth and
seventh degrees from the major scale of the tonic on which
our melody is based. Going down, the influence of the major
is withdrawn and we play the true minor scale. You will
notice that in the Chopin *Funeral March* the second and third
notes of the third phrase are descending, so the true minor
scale is used.

MELODIC MINOR SCALE ON A

When the minor scale is used to form chords, a compromise
is effected. Since a chord by itself does not show progress,
we do not know whether we are ascending or descending.
Therefore we have to decide definitely which degrees to use
in forming chords. We use the sixth note from the minor
scale and the seventh from the major. Notice that the variation in the minor scale only concerns the sixth and seventh
degrees; the first five and the octave are always those of the
true minor. The scale used to form chords is called the *harmonic minor* scale. If you play it on A, the only black note
you have to use is G sharp to produce the major seventh. It is
the same whether ascending or descending. Notice that the

interval between the sixth degree F and seventh G sharp is a tone and a half, larger than any other scale interval that we find and difficult to sing.

The variation of the upper part of the minor scale need not detain us at all. The important distinction between the major and minor mode is in the position of the third degree. Practice will soon sensitize the listener to the minor as distinct from the major third; the minor is perceptibly smaller and different in character. Audiences can usually distinguish between major and minor instinctively.

Now let us try a more difficult melody. Everyone knows *The Song of the Evening Star* from Wagner's opera *Tannhäuser*. Let us try it in the key of C also starting on C. Here is the rhythmic scheme of the first phrase:

You will find that white notes do not suffice and you will have to use some black ones. Although this phrase does not go above the fifth degree of the scale of C, you will have to use every half step within this interval with the exception of the one between C and D. We cannot tell from this phrase alone whether the melody is major or minor for it uses both the major and minor third. It appears to be based upon a scale beginning on C which uses every one of the twelve semitones into which the octave may be divided. This is called the *chromatic* scale. The chromatic scale has very little melodic value because every adjacent degree is at an equal interval from every other. Without the variety which comes from an arrangement of whole and half steps, the degrees of the

chromatic scale heard in succession are entirely lacking in the
melodic character which we found in the major and minor
modes. Therefore we seldom find melodies based on the chromatic scale. *The Evening Star* is really in major as we shall
find out if we play the entire melody. What happens is that
both major and minor melodies often borrow notes from the
chromatic scale as an added resource to melody. *Habanera*
from *Carmen* and Tosti's *Good Bye* both start out as if they
were based on the chromatic scale. Melodies employing many
chromatic notes we call *chromatic* in contradistinction to
those based entirely on the major or minor modes which are
called *diatonic*.

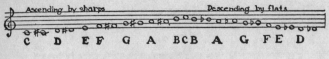

CHROMATIC SCALE

In the chapter on tone it was observed that some confusion
might be encountered in naming properly the notes represented by the black keys of the piano, since each black note
could be regarded as either a flat or a sharp. We found that if
we regarded them from the point of view of the scale, naming them proved to be logical and easy. Also we found that
the extra tones represented by the black notes came into existence so that we could reproduce or transpose the major
scale into any key. Now in the Pythagorean system of fixing
the intermediate tones of the octave, which served as the basis
of determining the exact pitch of the tones that we use, C
sharp, regarded as the third degree of the major scale of A, is
not the same note as D flat, which would be the third degree

of the minor scale of B flat. The two tones are near each other in pitch but if you should ask a violinist to play first C sharp and then D flat, you could hear the difference. The arrangement on the piano which conveniently fixes them as the same tone necessitates a total readjustment in our system of tuning known as the *tempered* scale.

Before the seventeenth century, when this system of tuning was adapted to them, keyboard instruments had much difficulty because the black notes did not always have the true pitch required by the scale in use. If the black note was tuned to play C sharp, it sounded false in a scale that called for D flat. The tempered scale solved this difficulty by redividing the octave into twelve equal semitones so that the difference between such degrees as C sharp and D flat was eliminated. Thus was produced the keyboard instrument of *equal temperament*. You have probably heard of the *Well-Tempered Clavichord,* a series of preludes and fugues in every key, major and minor, by Johann Sebastian Bach. This was published in 1722 and was intended to show that remote keys, formerly regarded as impractical because of tuning difficulties, were then available.

The tempered scale, although very familiar to us, is different from the *pure scale* and has not the ideal mathematical relationships conceived by Pythagoras. It has enormously simplified music and has laid the foundations for all modern composition. Nevertheless when left to our own devices without the piano to influence us, we still sing the pure scale and most instruments when not playing with piano do likewise. You can hear the difference between some of the notes of the two scales if you care to experiment. Strike C on the piano.

Now sing, do not play, C, D, E in succession. Hold the E and be sure you are in the middle of the tone. While you are still singing the tone, strike the E on the piano. You will find it perceptibly sharper than the E you are singing. Now sing the E again and compare the E on the piano. You will find that you have adjusted your tone to that of the instrument. Had you played C, D, E on the piano before singing, you would have sung the tempered E instinctively. It is an amazing proof of the subtlety of the human ear that this adjustment between the pure and tempered scale is so easily made. The degrees of the scale where the greatest difference between pure and tempered scale are to be found are the major and minor third, sixth and seventh. We speak of the relationship which makes C sharp and D flat identical by courtesy of equal temperament as an *enharmonic* one.

The major, minor and chromatic scales are not the only ones which are employed in modern music. During the last hundred years, composers have been experimenting with some of the other ancient modes. They do not fit in with our system of harmony so we seldom find compositions based entirely upon them. We do discover traces of them in certain melodies of Chopin, Liszt, Grieg and Brahms, as well as in composers nearer to our own time. These ancient scale relationships give a certain freshness to music and constitute an undoubted melodic resource. In modern music *artificial scales* are also found, that is, scale relationships unknown to our ancestors. The most familiar of these is the *whole-tone scale* which suppresses all half steps and reaches its octave on the seventh rather than on the eighth degree. Debussy used this scale frequently. The principal difficulty which it presents is that, like the chromatic succession of tones, it has not the variety found in the diatonic scales. Each interval is equally distant from its neighbor. Also it does not fit into our system of harmony. The whole-tone scale has proved somewhat of a boomerang in the hands of unskilful composers, bringing with it monotony rather than the desired freshness. At best it must be used with great reticence. Other synthetic scales such as those found in composers like Scriabin and Busoni have not reached the level of standardization. Their effect upon the ears of audiences is probably too confusing for ordinary use.

Melodies therefore always have a definite relationship to some accepted scale. They may borrow from other scales, they may even switch allegiance in passing from one phrase to another, or even in the middle of a phrase, but some definite relationship must exist if chaos is to be avoided and logical organization achieved.

We have not as yet found an answer to the interesting query as to what makes a melody beautiful. (By this we probably mean why do we happen to like a particular melody.) It is almost as difficult and useless a research as trying to discover why we like a particular friend. As in the case of the friend, we can usually discover certain admirable qualities which feed our esteem, but the lamentable fact remains that our affections sometimes center about thoroughly unadmirable people. The people we ought to like, we often despise. So, if a melody persists in appealing to us as beautiful, let us say that for us, it is beautiful. Do not forget however to apply the test of familiarity to see if its appeal is an enduring one.

Some of the admirable things which can be discovered in a

good melody are perfection of proportions, good rhythmic arrangement, a sense of climax, properly distributed cadences, clarity, variety of tones (too frequent reiteration of the same scale degree makes for dullness), and suitability to the performing medium. Even in the case of instrumental melodies, song-like quality is desirable. Tunes which sound well when discovered at the keyboard often appear in their true colors when we sing them. On the other hand, a melody which suits the voice rarely disappoints us when transferred to an instrumental medium.

If you are interested in distinguishing between a good and bad melody consider what one of the popular song writers did to the beautiful second theme found in the *Unfinished Symphony* of Schubert. It is called in the popular version, *My Song of Love*. It is a triumph of obviousness over subtlety.

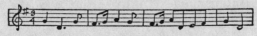

Theme from UNFINISHED SYMPHONY

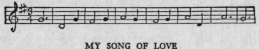

MY SONG OF LOVE

The composer changes the graceful subsidiary rhythms of Schubert to a heavy-footed affair with almost no variety of the primary rhythm. Also the little melodic twists that Schubert used in the succession of tones are carefully suppressed and ordinary melodic clichés are substituted.

If you wish to gain in melodic perception familiarize yourself with melodies from such masters as Mozart, Schubert and Chopin. Even in the composers who are less famous for tunes you will find that there are many melodies worth capturing. There is always some sort of melody in progress in a composition. Even the despised modern composer is more melodious than you have been led to think. Repetition of works by Stravinsky and Hindemith, for instance, may reveal melodies which have been concealed by the unfamiliar methods used by these composers.

An interesting thing happened in the case of one of the Preludes of Bach, the one in C major in volume one of the *Well-Tempered Clavichord*. This Prelude seems to consist only of a series of arpeggios or broken chords without any melody. However, when it is properly played, traces of a melody begin to appear in the top notes of each rhythmic group. Bach was giving us a very subtle effect, a suggested melody. But the French composer Gounod, who evidently liked his melodies unveiled, took this suggested melody of Bach and made it explicit with some additions of his own. This is known as the Bach-Gounod *Ave Maria*. Bach's original composition is relegated to the accompanying instrument and the Gounod melody is played or sung above it. Compare this with the effect as originally intended by Bach. You may agree with many musicians that his original plan is more interesting.

To sum up our findings, some sort of melody is present in every musical composition. We can discover it by playing the composition over and over until the melody takes shape in our consciousness. When we have finally captured it we may decide that we do not like it, or it may have worn out in the process. We may find it well worth the struggle that it caused us, and it will remain indefinitely with us, a source of great joy. The ultimate touchstone is our own taste. Incidental to the process of capturing the melody, we shall probably observe a number of interesting things about its rhythmic organization and its succession of tones. The more we observe, the more rapid will become our process of assimilation.

CHAPTER VI

Harmony

THE third element of musical arrangement is harmony. It may be defined as two or more tones of different pitch sounding simultaneously. Although the study of harmony involves many purely technical matters and is therefore somewhat more difficult for the layman than rhythm and melody, there are many interesting things for us to notice about it.

We shall observe that the harmonic structure of music varies enormously from the complex web of sounds of an orchestral piece to the simple melody accompanied by a few chords. If you consider the accompanying chords used for *Old Black Joe,* for instance, you will find that there are only three of them in all, and that in company with a host of amateur pianists, guitar and ukelele players you can readily find them by ear if you possess some degree of skill on an instrument.

If we focus our attention upon the harmonic aspect of music, whether it be simple or complex, we shall make two discoveries almost at once. In the first place, from the web of sound generally one melody will detach itself, so that we become conscious of the difference between melody and accompaniment. We shall notice secondly that the accompanying tones fashion themselves into simultaneous groups of notes or chords. These chords vary in the agreeableness of their sound when heard separately, but considered in succession seem to have logical arrangement.

Continuing our explorations along the line of the first discovery, we shall soon come to the conclusion that the principal melody is not always above the accompanying harmony. In Rubinstein's *Melody in F* and Liszt's *Liebestraum,* the melody first appears in the middle of the harmony, and in the case of *The Happy Farmer* of Schumann, the melody begins on the bottom with all the harmony above it. When we come to listen for melodies in symphonies, we shall not be at all surprised to discover the themes similarly located with respect to their accompaniments.

Next we shall perhaps be puzzled by the discovery that especially in piano music the chords accompanying the principal melody are not always sounded simultaneously. Chords may be broken so their notes are sounded in succession as in arpeggios, giving an effect of moving rather than of fixed harmony. You may have noticed that the harpist generally plays chords in this fashion. Although by definition this manner of playing a chord might be classified as melody rather than harmony, you will not be inclined to regard them as such because they have almost no melodic character.

Finally and most disconcerting of all, we shall gradually come to notice that although the accompanying sounds may be regarded as chords, sometimes they include melodies which are proceeding simultaneously with our principal melody. Consider a simple hymn tune such as *Holy, Holy, Holy.* We have already discovered that it is possible to regard the bass and alto parts as melodies although the sum total of the sounds they make, added to the soprano and the tenor, forms a series of chords. It is not so easy to detach melodies from the chords used to accompany *Old Black Joe,* but it is possible. Almost all harmony is so arranged that the chords are really the result of the combination of several melodies.

We must therefore conclude that harmony has two aspects, the vertical one, regarding each tone combination as a distinct musical impression, and the horizontal one, which deals with the separate melodies that go to make up the chords. The vertical aspect is the purely *harmonic* one; the horizontal one we call *counterpoint,* the science of melodic combination. A piece of music may contain each of these features equally stressed as in the case of the hymn tune mentioned above, or one feature may predominate. In the *Melody in F,* the chords have scarcely any horizontal or *contrapuntal* significance; in such a work as one of the great choruses from *The Messiah* of Handel, the contrapuntal element is more important than the harmonic. We shall study more of the combinations of melodies when we come to the chapter on polyphony. For the present our main concern is with the harmonic aspect of music.

Now let us pursue the second discovery which we made about harmony in general. Chords considered separately may either sound agreeable to our ears or may be relatively unpleasant. With our eighty-eight tones it is possible to find some extremely disagreeable combinations, even though we have reduced our tones to twelve by suppressing duplication in octaves. Sounds which are agreeable are called *consonant,* those which sound harsh *dissonant.* One may wonder why dissonance is tolerated in music. Would the ideal music furnish us with an unbroken series of consonances? This is a psychological problem easily related to the ordinary facts of life. The pleasures of this world are much more to be appreciated when they are alternated with a few pains. Hunger, which in itself is a very dissonant feeling, is relished when placed in juxtaposition to a good meal. In fact, we frequently court it, resorting to all manner of physical exertions to "work up an appetite." Fatigue often makes going to bed a much more desirable experience than it normally would be. We never enjoy good health fully until we have been deprived of it for a time.

Music operates in the same fashion. If we were to have nothing but consonance we should soon become sleepy and bored. There would be no incentive to progress. Dissonance, providing the disagreeable sound, drives music onward to new sounds in the hope that things will improve. We speak of dissonances *resolving* into consonances. This means a dissonant chord is followed by a consonant one according to definite harmonic principles. The skilful relationship of these two elements makes for effective harmonic background. It is a well-known psychological fact that disagreeable sounds sometimes improve as we become accustomed to them. The history of music shows that with the development of the art, human ears have adjusted themselves to increasingly complex harmonic combinations. What was regarded as dissonant by one age, is philosophically accepted or even liked by a later one. We shall find therefore that the more recent the music, the greater degree of dissonance included. Fashions change in harmony so rapidly that music which was adequate for one era sounds hopelessly outmoded in another. Only the music of those composers who wrote with sufficient inspiration to rise above the fashions of the times has been preserved for our ears. This also explains why audiences are rather slow to accept contemporary music. Composers are usually more sensitive to new sounds than listeners. As a result they may include harmonic effects in their works which are sufficiently dissonant to make the music appear distasteful. After a time, when the sounds have become more familiar, it is much easier to estimate the value of the music. You may have had the experience of discovering one day that you liked a piece of music which you had always thought harsh and unpleasant. This could probably be explained in terms of the above-mentioned adjustment of the ear to new sounds.

It would be profitable to examine compositions of Palestrina, Handel, Haydn, Beethoven, Chopin, Wagner, Ravel and Stravinsky in turn, in order to notice the gradual increase of dissonant harmony. Bach is not included in this list because his music was much more daring in harmonic combinations than that of his contemporaries; he anticipated many effects undiscovered in general practice until many years later.

Chord succession provides for the logical relationship of one chord to another. Consonances are planned to succeed dissonances, and the division of the music into phrases, which we have seen is accomplished by rhythmic grouping and melodic cadence, is much aided by cadence of harmony. As in the case of a melody, suspense and repose, calculated to sustain the interest but not overburden the sustaining powers of the mind, are characteristic of a balanced progression of chords. For the end of a phrase we need a feeling of cadence, but not to such a degree that the interest is not carried over to the next phrase. For the end of a group of phrases constituting an entire melody, a final cadence bringing with it a sense of completion is desirable.

We have two sorts of harmonic cadences, *suspensive* and *conclusive*. The suspensive cadence is rarely a dissonant combination of tones for this would not provide any feeling of repose; on the other hand it will necessarily differ from the final cadence or the interest will flag. Suppose we examine the cadences of *Old Black Joe* to see what contribution the harmony makes to the division of phrases. It has been remarked that only three chords are used to accompany this melody, so we shall not find much subtlety of harmonic cadence. Notice that the first chord is used also for the endings of the first, third and fourth phrases. The second phrase ending, which contains one of the other chords, is more suspensive than that of the others. However, the first and third phrases do not give the entire effect of a conclusive cadence. The melody is partly responsible for this for, as we have seen, the fifth note of the scale which serves as the melodic ending of these two phrases has not the cadence feeling of the tonic found at the conclusion of the last phrase. But there is another explanation of the variety of cadence feeling between the first and last phrase endings, a purely harmonic one. Notice that in the first ending a different chord precedes the final one; this is responsible for the difference in effect. The progression of chords represented by the last two of *Old Black Joe* is the strongest and most definite cadence of harmony. It is almost universally used where a strong ending is desired. We call it the *authentic* cadence. If you will test a number of song endings, you will find that the authentic cadence is almost always found at the end of the last phrase.

The cadence represented by the last two chords of the first and third phrases is sometimes used as an alternative to the authentic cadence where such a strong ending is not desired. It is known as the *plagal* cadence. You will find it used as the "amen" for most hymn tunes. The tunes generally conclude by an authentic cadence but are followed by the less emphatic plagal cadence serving as amen. The cadence of the second phrase ending is definitely suspensive.

You will often find the authentic cadence in the middle of a simple folk tune but not usually combined with a masculine ending on the tonic. When all factors unite to furnish cadence feeling, it is difficult for the music to proceed. An example of this is the ending of the first phrase of *America* where we find the tonic in the melody, a masculine ending and an authentic cadence. You may observe that the song as a result seems divided rather arbitrarily into two sections.

Another familiar song which college students often sing is the Latin Ode *Integer Vitae*. Here is the rhythmic scheme to refresh your memory:

You will observe that the rhythmic scheme contains some subtlety; there are feminine endings of the first three phrases, no two phrases are exactly alike, and the fourth phrase is shorter than the others.

If you can recall the harmony or get someone to play it for you, you will find that each harmonic cadence is suspensive and different from every other, and that the only authentic cadence is that of the final phrase. From this analysis you will have an explanation of the sustained effect of this song, much superior harmonically to the other songs we have analysed.

Perhaps you would like a few technical explanations of the phenomena of consonance and dissonance and of harmonic cadence. In music the final appeal is to the ear, and you may easily be content to observe that these qualities exist in harmony without attempting to find out why. Science sometimes has a hard time catching up with facts which are understood instinctively; in the history of harmonic science, the theorists are always several steps behind the composers. Our principles of harmony were not definitely established before the time of Bach, and even nineteenth-century philosophers like Schopenhauer and Helmholtz had different explanations to offer of familiar musical phenomena.

Let us begin with consonance and dissonance and limit our consideration for the moment to the combination of two sounds. You will find that every note of the scale combined with the tonic has a recognizable sound often heard in harmony; these combinations vary greatly in consonance. We call them the *intervals of the scale;* they take their names from the scale degree combined with the tonic. Therefore two tonics combined give a *unison,* the second degree with the tonic gives the interval of the *second,* the third and tonic, the interval of the *third* and so on up to the octave. We may also form intervals using the minor scale, but be sure and select the true minor, that is the series of white notes beginning on A without the alterations employed by the melodic minor scale when ascending.

If you compare the intervals of the major scale for consonance you will agree that after the unison the octave is most consonant. Of the others you will be fairly sure that the seventh in the major scale is the most dissonant, the second somewhat less so. Musicians agree that the order from consonance to dissonance is octave, fifth, fourth, third, sixth, second and seventh. You may feel inclined to place the third higher in consonance than the fourth or fifth because we have become so accustomed to the sound of it from melodies which are harmonized throughout by accompanying thirds. However, the Middle Ages did not even admit that the third was a consonance but regarded it as a dissonance, requiring resolution to the fifth or the unison. In modern music we call it a consonance but place it lower than the fourth and fifth.

It would be of great value to your ear if you would learn to distinguish the intervals one from the other. The difficult ones to determine will probably be the fourth, fifth and sixth; the rest are easy.

Three explanations have been made of the difference in consonance of the intervals of the scale according to Pole in *The Philosophy of Music.* The first one is that in the case of consonant sounds, "preference is due to the simplicity of the ratios between the vibration-numbers of the two limiting sounds." He gives the following tables showing these ratios for consonances and dissonances:

consonances		*dissonances*	
OCTAVE	2:1	MAJOR SECOND	9:8
FIFTH	3:2	MAJOR SEVENTH	15:8
FOURTH	4:3	MINOR "	16:9
MAJOR THIRD	5:4	TRITONE	45:32
MINOR "	6:5		
MAJOR SIXTH	5:3		
MINOR "	8:5		

The tritone is the interval between the fourth and seventh degrees of the major scale, so called because it is a fourth separated by three whole tones. The perfect fourth is two tones and a semitone apart. The tritone has always been regarded as a very dissonant interval.

A second explanation was offered by Rameau, the great French composer who was a contemporary of Bach. Rameau observed that the first four consonances appear in the same order in the system of harmonics. Since they are present in every sound, they naturally are harmonious. You will recall that starting with the C below middle C, the first harmonic is the *octave* above, the second the *fifth* above that (G), the third, two octaves above the fundamental, a C, which is also a *fourth* above the preceding harmonic, and the fourth is a *third* above the later (E). This explanation is ingenious but runs into difficulties if we attempt to carry it into the higher harmonics.

The third explanation is that of Helmholtz. It is summed up as follows by Pole: "When two notes are sounded together, the harmonics or overtones of each are liable to interfere with each other, producing a certain roughness or harshness and it is the greater or less liability to this which influences the smoothness of the combination, and gives it the character of a more or less consonant interval." Without attempting to discuss this explanation at length, we may observe that two tones which have a majority of their overtones in common naturally will tend to greater consonance than two tones whose partial tones are entirely different.

When we come to consider combinations of three or more tones we shall find that our system of overtones also gives us a basic chord which sounding simultaneously as every tone is produced is really a chord of nature; it is formed from the first four harmonics and is called the *common* or *tonic* chord. As the tonic note of the scale is the central point of melody so the common chord formed on the scale is the central part of the harmonic system. Turning again to *Old Black Joe* we find that the chord which begins and ends the song is that of C, E, G, the tonic chord of C. This combination is also called the *major triad* of C. A triad may be formed by taking the first, third and fifth degrees of any ascending series of eight tones. We can therefore easily find the minor triad of C or of any other scale.

By forming triads beginning on each degree of the scale of C, using, however, only the tones of the C major scale, we shall discover that there are six other triads possible in this key. Of these, the triads of the fourth and fifth degrees have major thirds like the tonic triad. The triads of the second, third and sixth degrees have minor thirds and therefore sound like minor triads. The triad formed on the seventh degree of the scale has a minor third and the interval of the fifth is a half tone too small to produce a perfect fifth. We call this interval a diminished fifth and the chord a *diminished triad*.

TRIADS OF THE C MAJOR SCALE

Because of their similarity of sound to that of the tonic triad, the triads on the fifth and fourth degree seem most closely related to it and in fact they are. Before you make an interesting experiment you should understand that the notes of the triad retain their combined harmonic value no matter how they are arranged. Duplication on the octave, inversion so that the third or the fifth is the lowest note, does not change the character of the chord. You can play the common chord in many different positions, thanks to the seven octaves of the piano keyboard. Begin your experiment by hunting out some of the many positions which this chord may take. So long as you use only these three tones or their octave duplicates, you may play as many notes as you have fingers, or with an arpeggio, make all registers of the keyboard sound; you still are dealing only with the C major chord. Now arrange the triad which you found on G in similar fashion and try a succession of the G triad followed by the tonic chord. You have found the authentic cadence. In similar fashion try a succession between the triad of the fourth degree, F, followed by the tonic. Here is the plagal cadence. With these three chords you can provide the accompaniment to *Old Black Joe*.

If you arrange the various triads well, you will find that

you can improvise accompaniments to many other songs, not limiting yourself to three chords but experimenting with some of the other triads which also may be used to accompany melodies in the key of C.

Each note of the scale has a name as well as a number, and the triads take their names from these:

1st	degree	*tonic*	5th	degree	*dominant*
2nd	degree	*super-tonic*	6th	degree	*sub-mediant*
3rd	degree	*mediant*	7th	degree	*leading tone*
4th	degree	*sub-dominant*			

The authentic cadence is therefore produced by the tonic chord preceded by the dominant triad. The plagal cadence is a succession from the sub-dominant triad to the tonic chord. Aside from their similarity of sound to that of the tonic triad, it is hard to explain the cadence feeling and close relationship which they have to the tonic. Rameau attempted to explain this in terms of a system which he called "Fundamental Bass." Each chord has as a root the fundamental tone which produced it. These roots or fundamental bass notes have a tendency to move to the nearest non-duplicating harmonic. Accordingly, G with its common chord is the nearest relative to the C triad. We observe then that the G triad may be regarded as either the dominant triad of C or the tonic triad of G. In the case of the relation of C to F or tonic to sub-dominant, we reverse our relationship; C is the nearest relative to F and hence the C and F triads most naturally succeed each other but with somewhat less emphasis than in the relationship between C and G, when viewed from the aspect of the key of C.

These technical explanations of harmony are only an introduction to its serious study. It is the branch of music which has been most recently developed and while it has enormously increased the expressive powers of music, we must not forget that our system is the only one which includes harmony at all. Much of our early music was unharmonized and even today we have lovely examples of unharmonized melody such as the English Horn solo at the beginning of the third act of *Tristan and Isolda,* or the song which Mélisande sings at the window while combing her hair, from Debussy's beautiful opera. The listener should learn to appreciate also the music of the ancient church, Gregorian chant, where, by its very nature, harmonic accompaniment is precluded. Since the development of harmony as witnessed by all music since the sixteenth century, our melodies have come more and more to depend upon harmony for their completion, and oftentimes lose all significance when presented without it.

The duty of the listener to harmony should be first to distinguish between melodies and accompanying harmonies. Hunt out the melodies wherever they are. This will be easy in piano music which is more often harmonic than contrapuntal; not so easy, though, in listening to a symphony. A good plan when at an orchestral concert is to pay particular attention to some instrument which is not playing the principal melody. Notice the second violins or the cellos and see if you can follow what they are playing. It may be only part of the harmony and have little melodic significance but it is almost sure to have some melodic character.

Notice, too, the part harmony plays in cadence; see if you can recognize the types of cadence and can tell the difference between harmony based upon the major and the minor mode. Consider, too, the part dissonance plays in chord progression and watch for the resolutions of dissonant chords into consonances. Unless you happen to be hearing a piece of such a contemporary figure as Schoenberg, who is almost pedantic in his avoidance of consonance, you will find consonance appearing agreeably in the wake of the dissonant harmonies.

CHAPTER VII

Design in Music

IN the chapter on the language of music, we discovered that all music consists of two elements, expression and design. The expressive part we found to be inexact, personal and subjective both from the composer's and the auditor's point of view. We found that it requires no analysis and that it is most enjoyable when accepted instinctively. Design, on the other hand, is an exact language which must be understood to be appreciated in full. We have examined closely the elements which enter into musical design; tone, its selection and production, rhythm, melody and harmony.

It hardly seems necessary to argue the necessity for design in any art. We have probably had some experiences where consciousness of bad design caused us to lose our fondness for a work of art. Perhaps you can recall liking a picture very much which hung on the wall of your room. Then one day someone who was conscious of design came along and pointed out to you that while the details of drawing were correct, the arrangement of the figures made an ugly pattern. Once this had been pointed out to you, you never enjoyed the picture again so much. Eventually you probably replaced it by another. This time you may have been more critical in your selection. You were beginning to know something about pictures.

You may not agree that the connoisseur who pointed out to you the faulty design did you a good turn. It might have been better to go on enjoying the picture in your simple unquestioning attitude. Undoubtedly it would have been better if he had made you enjoy the picture more by showing you, provided there were any, the good points of the design. It is all a matter of your feeling for education. The person who wants to be educated is willing to have his feelings hurt occasionally if thereby he can enjoy more subtly and more extensively.

Regardless of whether we choose to appreciate design instinctively, and everyone has something of the instinct, or with the trained eye, history proves to us that a work of good design will outlive its inferior. More people today may prefer an example of magazine cover portraiture to a picture of Titian or a ballad of Irving Berlin to a song of Schumann, but over a space of years Titian and Schumann would easily win the competition. The difference in inspiration must of course be taken into account, but that is difficult to measure. Differences of design are immediately apparent. Even a work of the highest inspiration will lose in value if it has faults of design; conversely, a much less valuable idea may last for years if it is superlatively presented.

In many of the arts it is difficult to isolate pure design because it is so bound up with representation. For instance, in a painting, design usually can only play a secondary rôle to the more apparent one of the reproduction of landscapes, persons and so on. Modern painters have made many experiments in pure design without much encouragement from the public. Similarly in architecture, design is involved with all manner of practical considerations such as solidity, admission of light, disposition of interiors, and so on. We find examples of almost pure design in such things as church towers, which are intended less for usefulness than for ornament. Interesting variations of symmetry are to be found in the treatment of the towers in Gothic cathedrals. Also some delightful schemes for repetition are to be found in some traditional styles of housebuilding. There is a typical Long Island farmhouse, for instance, which consists of a small replica of the larger part adjacent to it. This is not particularly useful to the building scheme and it certainly is not economical, but it is very pleasing as design.

Music intended to accompany words or to embody a program may be as hampered in design as painting or architecture if its construction is influenced by the poem or story. Therefore, we find that instrumental music without descriptive titles affords us the best opportunity to study musical design. Such music is in reality pure design, for nothing but musical considerations enter into the general scheme of composition. Among musicians there is generally to be found a prejudice in favor of so-called *absolute music* in which the design is submitted to no extra-musical influences. It must be about something definite and must be logical in its arrangement, but that something is entirely musical in character.

The design of absolute music is frequently of large extent as, for instance, the form used in the first movement of a symphony. Let us compare this to the general plan of an essay. An essay begins with its subject stated in the first paragraph. Following this will come related material and its bearing upon the central theme will be indicated. The thought will then be developed and conclusions reached. The last part of the essay will usually contain a restatement of the central idea. In the symphony, the first movement form, as found in such composers as Beethoven or Brahms, begins with the statement of a central musical subject; subsidiary themes are introduced after appropriate transition. There follows a development of themes singly or in combination, restatement of themes and conclusion. Here is a form which is both definite and logical. It is surely not the ideal one for us to select to begin our study of musical design, for it is the most elaborate pattern which has been evolved in the history of music.

Let us commence with the folk song, which, although it cannot be included in the category of absolute music, because it is associated with words, has a very definite musical design. This design embodies the principle of simple repetition such as we find in textiles and wall papers, with the fundamental difference, however, that folk songs have a definite beginning and ending. Wall papers more closely resemble the primitive designs of savages in which a single musical phrase is repeated indefinitely.

Folk songs are short musical settings of popular verse. They are often of uncertain origin. Since they were usually unrecorded and passed on from singer to singer they suffered many changes, somewhat in the nature of a smoothing-out process. They bear the imprint of the feeling of the people for simple melody. As a result they are often so perfect in design as to be practically indestructible. Certainly they represent one of our great musical heritages.

The folk song generally consists of one stanza of music repeated for each stanza of the verse. Such repetition is often prejudicial to the dramatic values of the poem. Take for instance *Barbara Allen,* based upon the tragic story of a young man who loved a hard-hearted and capricious lady. In fact he loved her so much that her unresponsiveness brought him into a dying condition. When friends urged her to come to his bedside and cheer him up, she reluctantly appeared and made the casual observation; "Young man, I see you're dyin'." This cruel act brought about her own downfall; she went into a decline and shortly thereafter died. The appropriate and traditional dispositions of the graves were made by the surviving village maidens. This tragic story has variations of mood and intensity which could well be shown by the music, but the repetition of four short melodic phrases provides a somewhat inadequate setting. Musical considerations influence this repetition and the dramatic values are subordinated. This type of song with single repeated stanza we call the *strophic* song.

When words and music are joined together one or the other dominates the design. The strophic song, in which dramatic values suffer, has as its opposite the *recitative,* which pays scant attention to musical values. It amounts practically to a recitation to music; none of the repetition so necessary to musical design appears in it. Opera is generally a compromise between recitative, embodying the plot and uninteresting musically, and set musical pieces which interfere with the plot but are musically satisfying. Music is very dictatorial when it is associated with any other art; either it must have its own instinct for design satisfied or it goes off into vague meanderings which even a well-designed poem or drama cannot support. Excepting the recitative, therefore, all music with words will generally be found to contain a recognized musical design. The folk song with its strophic pattern and frequent repetition of phrases in a single stanza is only one instance of this.

Unity of musical design is brought about by choice of key, by rhythm, by literal repetition of parts or the whole of a melodic phrase, by harmony or similarity of accompaniment. Variety is shown in modifications of these. Naturally enough the longer the piece, the more variety we shall find. Too much repetition makes for monotony, too much variety for incoherence. If you have ever heard someone who insists upon enlivening his surroundings by singing a song called *Abdul, a Bul Bul Ameer* with what appears to be hundreds of repetitions of the single stanza of a dreary waltz, you will agree as to the monotony. But the long chaotic effect of an operatic recitative would be almost as dull. We need our unity and variety nicely proportioned.

Let us examine some simple four-phrase folk songs which we have probably sung many times without a thought to their proportions. One which contains almost a maximum of literal repetition within a single stanza is *Drink To Me Only With Thine Eyes*. In fact you will discover that of the four phrases only the third differs at all. The first, second and fourth come to a full cadence upon the tonic. This inclusion of three full cadences in a four-phrase song is seldom found. Six-eight time with the value of a triplet on each half of the bar would make each phrase four bars long. All the endings are masculine except that of the third phrase where we have the pleasant variety contributed by a feminine ending and a suspensive cadence on the dominant. Notice how welcome this third phrase is when it appears. If you were to suppress the third phrase and substitute still another repetition of the other, the effect would be intolerable. Perhaps you will find that there is a little too much repetition anyway for your taste. Still the poem is so beautiful and the initial phrase of the song so melodious that we find the song an agreeable musical design.

Let us adopt some symbols so that we can chart similarity of phrases in shortened form. Suppose we use the same letter for each repetition of melodic phrase, and a different one when there is a change. In phrases where the beginning of the melody is the same but the ending different, use the same letter to the first, second or third power as may be necessary. Similarity of rhythm, to avoid confusion, we shall have to note in longhand. *Drink To Me* then would be charted AABA. B has an anacrusis, a feminine ending and a suspensive cadence. The rhythm also changes somewhat in disposition of accents. The melody is noticeably different.

Believe Me If All Those Endearing Young Charms has slightly more variety than this. You will discover that though the first, second and fourth phrases are much alike, we shall have to chart it as AA′BA′. The reason for this is that the two A primes have endings designed to bring the melody to a full close on the tonic. A ends on the third degree of the scale with an effect partially suspensive, although the harmony is the tonic chord. This you can see is a little more subtle in design. As in the case of the other song the time signature will be 6/8 and there will be four bars to a phrase. There is an anacrusis at the beginning of each phrase and the endings are all masculine. Notice that although B has some variety of melody, it ends upon the same note as A, the third degree with tonic harmony and partially suspensive cadence.

The verse of *Old Black Joe* affords us still more variation although the effect is simple. Here the scheme is AA'AB. The cadence at A which brings the fifth degree of the scale and tonic harmony, is less suspensive than the one in A' where the melody ends on the second degree of the scale and uses dominant harmony. B is entirely different melodically and ends on the tonic. The endings are all masculine and there is an anacrusis only on B. If you go on to the chorus you will find two additional phrases; the first contains a new melodic idea for the words "I'm comin'." This is heard twice and then the phrase concludes with exactly the same ending that is used in A. The last phrase is a literal repetition of B. The chorus would be charted CB.

We have already remarked that *The Londonderry Air* has four phrases which are exactly alike in rhythm but different melodically. We should chart this AA'BC, a lettering which does not do justice to the fine unity of the song. This unity is obtained by repeating the rhythm with a gradual rising of the melodic inflection embodying it. Each phrase could be subdivided into two parts. The first part of A is precisely similar to that of A', the endings change to admit a suspensive cadence in A and a conclusive one in A'. The thing that surprises us about the song is that instead of a repetition of A' at the end, we have a new melody which rises to the greatest climax of the song. Musically this makes a more interesting effect, for there is undoubtedly plenty of unity and yet we feel that we have progressed somewhere in the unfolding of the melody.

Another interesting kind of repetition is found in *America*. We must call the two phrases AB for they are different melodically. A rhythmic fragment, however, revealed in the first two measures is repeated over and over in the course of the song. It is from this fragmentary repetition that unity is derived. We may be surprised to discover that such a simple tune as *America* should be based upon so subtle a design. It shows us that the unity which comes from the repetition of a rhythmic fragment is very effective. We shall find this device used very often in much larger forms.

It would be well if, before proceeding further in your study of design, you should study many more folk songs. It is excellent practice for the ear to think through a song with no help from an instrument or your voice. If you are willing to make the effort, you will probably find that it is not only easy but agreeable to imagine in its entirety the sound of a short piece. In this way, your memory will receive valuable training. Try and chart the pieces you have so imagined and note down details of rhythm and melody as well as the phrase arrangement.

If you feel prepared to go further, let us examine now some simple instrumental music. Probably our memories are not up to the effort of recreating these pieces in the imagination. A phonograph record would be an excellent aid to further study, or if you can play the works on the piano yourself, so much the better. Let us select, to begin with, Schumann's popular *Träumerei*. This was written as a piano piece, but it is often heard transcribed for violin or cello with piano accompaniment or for organ. It does not matter for our purposes whether or not you play the original or transcribed arrangement. The design remains unaltered. Play the piece through several times without attempting analysis. You will find that the melody is a very appealing one which appears to have considerable repetition but is not at all monotonous. Now see if you can divide it into phrases. This will not be difficult for you will notice that there are cadences at the end of each phrase and that each phrase begins with the same anacrusis. There are eight phrases in all, the first two are literally repeated. Notice that there is only one full cadence in the entire piece and that this comes properly enough at the end. Now let us see if we can chart the eight phrases. AA'AA'A''A''' AA'''' is fairly accurate. You may not agree with the lettering of the sixth phrase as A'''. It begins with the same melodic figure as the others but uses different degrees of the scale. Such repetition we call repetition by *transposition,* or changing the tonal level of the melody. Since the disposition of the notes is the same we are perhaps justified in using the same letter.

Our chart shows us that Schumann obtains unity by repeating the beginning of his melody in every phrase, and variety by changing the rest of it frequently. It might be profitable to inquire why Schumann used transposition of the melody in the sixth phrase. Was it merely for the sake of variety? Let us play through the piece again and see if we can discover any other reason. How about climax? Isn't it advisable for a melody to make a curve in the disposition of its phrases so

that there is a high and a low point? If there is a continual
level of interest in a long melody we find it rather wearying.
Undoubtedly this sixth phrase gives the effect of a climax for
the whole piece. The other phrases all have climaxes, but in
comparison with these the entire sixth phrase sounds more
important. Why? Simply because the whole melody is stated
on a higher level. As tones rise, we invariably experience a
growth in intensity of feeling. This sixth phrase becomes the
most important feature of the design.

Now let us examine the rhythm. Schumann is a very subtle
composer who seems to delight in seeking out unusual rhythmic effects. We can sense at once that the rhythm is duple
but the subsidiary rhythm is harder to analyse. He uses the
metrical scheme of 4/4 providing for lesser and greater
accents in a single bar, but the effect of his rhythm is quite
different. Here is the rhythmical plan of the first phrase:

Notice that on beat *three* of the first bar after the anacrusis,
no note is struck to parallel the metrical accent, but that there
are three short notes immediately thereafter. In the second
and fourth bars a still more unusual effect is found, the disposition of the melody is to accent the second rather than the
first beat. The melody and the harmony both assist the second
beat to become more important than the first. This gives the
effect of syncopation. We should not be surprised to find
syncopation in a lively melody, but in one which is smooth
and lyric in effect, such a device seems almost perverse. In
fact this rhythmic idea is what gives *Träumerei* its character

and originality. When you come to analyse your feelings about the piece, you will realize that it is this very feature which you like best and will remember. If you try to beat the time as the piece proceeds you will see that it is rather difficult to do.

With such a subtle rhythmic effect to convey to our minds, Schumann is justified in using considerable repetition in order that the design shall be clear. In every phrase the rhythm is practically identical; you will find in the fourth bar of some of the phrases a slight variation, but that is all the change that occurs. In the last phrase there is a high note in the melody, almost on the level of the one found in the sixth phrase. This is a subsidiary climax which Schumann underlines by marking a hold over the note. The rhythm momentarily is suspended while the effect of the note is felt. A *ritardando* or slowing up gives an air of finality to the ending of the last phrase.

We can now parallel what must have been Schumann's method in composing this piece. He may not have analysed each step as we are compelled to do, but his trained instinct must have taken him over the same ground. Here was, to begin with, a melodic idea with an unusual rhythmical complexion. Because it was so unusual, much repetition was necessary to make it clear. Accordingly he planned to repeat the rhythm in a number of phrases but at the same time to vary the effect by changing the top note to which the melody ascended. The whole sixth phrase was transposed to a higher level. This gave him not only variety but climax. He used a suspensive cadence at the end of every phrase except the last, and made the endings feminine so that, in spite of much symmetry, the piece would be impelled forward. The net result is a design of apparent simplicity but great perfection and originality.

Now let us examine a somewhat longer piano piece, *Humoresque* by the Czech composer, Dvořák. This also exists in different versions. It is very popular as transcribed for violin and piano. A first playing of the record reveals that we have much more variety of material than in the Schumann piece. It also seems to consist of more than one mood. Play it over several times without attempting a definite analysis. There is much symmetry immediately apparent. The melody which begins the piece comes back a number of times. In fact it seems to appear in full and with but slight change three times. In addition to this, it is repeated at the very beginning. We find that to letter the whole piece in groups of similar phrases, we shall have to use these symbols, ABA′CA″B′. C appears to be quite long and has a great deal of repetition in it. Also you may have noticed that it is in minor, whereas A and B are both in major. It is almost like a piece in itself. Except for its final cadence which is suspensive, it might stand entirely alone. Accordingly to simplify our analysis, suppose we divide the piece into sections, a first part made up of AB, a middle, C, and an ending, AB. This seems to make the whole piece a sort of ABA in form. The third part is almost exactly like the first with suppression of some repetitions, and the middle part is entirely different.

This brings us to a very familiar device of composers. Variety and unity are sought not only from phrase to phrase, but from section to section. Folk songs and short piano pieces consist of only one section, but longer pieces are usually easily divisible into several. The arrangement of a composition into three sections according to the ABA plan is so common as to be called the fundamental plan of musical arrangement. If you listen carefully to the first section of any composition, you will almost surely recognize and hear all this material repeated again after an excursion into some different music for a middle section. The large ABA plan is sometimes called *Song-Form*. You can see its relationship to the usual AABA form of the folk song. In the folk song the introductory phrase is usually repeated for the sake of clarity, then there is a digression followed by a repetition of the first phrase. In the large song-form we shall find that the sections usually bear this relationship one to another as well as in their constituent phrases.

Let us go back to the first section of *Humoresque*. Suppressing the literal repetition of the first two phrases we find six different phrases arranged in this order of appearance: AA'BB'AA''. This is a plan often found in folk songs. With the repetitions there are eight phrases arranged in this fashion: AA'AA'BB'AA''. There is a slight change in the ending of A'' which we may not have noticed before. This change, after several repetitions of the original, brings an added expressiveness, but it is very slight.

Each phrase is exactly four bars long. The rhythm is duple and is stated in simple 2/4 meter. The difference between A and A' is one of cadence, A' being conclusive and A being suspensive. The rhythmical character of A is derived from a series of long and short notes used alternately with rests in between. It is a very simple scheme, but the movement of the melody ascending and descending in each phrase makes it interesting.

B and B′ change the rhythm and reverse the order of cadence, B being conclusive and feminine and B′ suspensive so as to lead us naturally back to A. B is a more smoothly flowing melody harmonized closely by a parallel voice mostly in thirds. Its expressive character depends chiefly upon this harmonization. Suppress the second voice and you will find the melody much less effective.

The section ends with a conclusive cadence and the tonic harmony. We immediately enter the middle section with the change to minor mode and slower tempo. This section also consists of four phrases which can be lettered AA′A″A‴. Each phrase is readily divided into two bars, but really consists of four bars. The difference between A and A′ is one of cadence although they are both suspensive. A″ is like A with the addition of a little melodic ornamentation for expressive reasons, and A‴ is like A″ with a fuller accompaniment and the melody in octaves. There is not a full cadence in the whole section. In this way the interest is made to move forward so that we unconsciously await the return of the first section.

The first section, when it appears again, suppresses all repeats and gives us this plan: AA″BB″. You will notice that we have not had B″ before, but it is a modification of the ending of B′ so as to provide a full cadence and an ending of the whole piece.

By a close attention to the analysis of *Humoresque*, you will be surprised to discover how well you can follow the design of an extended piece. When the elements are understood and clearly heard, and when we know from a knowledge of familiar musical patterns what to expect, our ears will give us very accurate understanding of the language of musical design.

In the third section of *Humoresque* we noted that the suppression of repetitions contained in the first prevented the two sections from being absolutely symmetrical. There are two good reasons for this. When material is being introduced by the composer, there is a need of repetition to impress it upon the ear of the listener. Such repetition coming later in the course of the piece is both unnecessary and tedious. We shall therefore usually find the third sections of song-form, if the material is the same, somewhat shorter. There is another good reason for change in the third section. Perfect symmetry, which is obtained by a literal repetition of the third section by the first, produces a design which is somewhat static. We like to feel in the unfolding of a composition that there has been some progress in thought.

Accordingly we shall discover that, even in the simple song-form, the third section will often change so as to reflect development of the musical thought. Not only will needless repetition of phrases be omitted, but phrases of the melody will be given new and more significant turns. A good example of such a design is the *Song* from Edward MacDowell's *Sea Pieces*. Section one contains two melodic ideas, A and B, arranged in the order ABA. Section two has two new ideas, C, which is stated in the left hand with accompaniment above, and D, a lyric melody in the top voice. These are arranged CDC. In the last section the material of D is incorporated into the last repetition of A, replacing the former second phrase of A. In other respects the arrangement of the material in sections one and three is similar, with only slight changes to increase the sonority of B.

You will probably encounter little difficulty in following the simple three-part song-form. Let us experiment with a longer and more closely unified composition, the *Adagio Cantabile* from Beethoven's *Sonata Pathétique,* Opus 13. At a first hearing you will notice that it is based upon a lyric melody of great beauty, and that this melody makes three different appearances. In between the sections in which it appears, there is contrasting material. Now examine the three sections devoted to the principal melody and note their differences. The first time it is heard the lower register of the piano is used, followed by repetition in the octave above. The second time it appears only once, and in the lower register. The third time it occurs in both registers but the effect is different because the accompanying figure has a changed rhythm. Notice that this rhythm increases the intensity of the music; groups of three, or triplets, have succeeded the easy flowing two groups.

Indicating the appearances of the melody as sections one, three, and five, let us examine sections two and four. Section two consists of a different melody and a different accompaniment. Massed chords are used instead of a broken figure, but they are still in groups of two. This section is not independently interesting, but seems to drive the music forward as well as to provide contrast. Section four is more interesting. There is a new melody in the upper voice which is answered by a melody in the lower voice, the accompaniment appearing between them. Notice the rhythm of this accompaniment; it is the first appearance of the triplet figure which, once introduced, continues in combination with the original melody of the first section.

We have then five sections, one, three, and five devoted to the melody, two and four providing contrast, and, in the case of four, new material to be incorporated in the main design. At the end of each of the even-numbered sections there is preparation for the return of the original melody.

After the cadence of the melody in the fifth section, notice that the composition does not immediately end. There are added seven bars to form a short concluding section, containing a new melody which appears to grow out of the principal melody. Such an appended section, which adds to the feeling of completion, we call a *coda*.

This composition, by the master architect, Beethoven, will probably be more difficult to follow than the preceding examples given, but a few hearings should make it clear. When you have listened to it carefully and grasped its significance, you will realize that the logic of the design enhances the beauty of the musical material.

In listening to long pieces it is difficult even for the trained musician to perceive details of variation with a single hearing. We have made a close analysis of these four pieces to show what happens in the course of their development, how they are made to achieve variety, unity and logical progress. Such close analysis is only profitable for study. Do not feel that to appreciate music properly you must be able to repeat this analysis of everything you hear. As you progress you will find that you are instinctively aware of repetition and variation of material. When this happens so naturally that you still have a portion of attention left to devote to the subjective, emotional side of the music, you may be entitled to feel that you understand something of the language of music.

CHAPTER VIII

Tonality

IN the last chapter while discussing unity and variety, mention was made of choice of key as contributing to design. Naturally if a composition is based entirely upon a given major or minor scale, a certain amount of unity is achieved. Is it possible or advisable to use more than one key in a single work? Let us examine the most elaborate form, the symphony. We have already noticed that the symphony consists of several pieces or movements. Do these pieces all use the same key? Perhaps we can tell from their titles. The Third Symphony of Beethoven, the *Eroica,* also is called the Symphony in E flat major; the Fifth Symphony of the same composer is called Symphony in C minor. Evidently the title tells us the key and mode of the work. Let us look at the second movement of the Symphony in E flat, the *Funeral March.* This is not in E flat at all; it is not even in major. It seems to be in C minor. The second movement of the C minor Symphony is in A flat major. If the keys of the different movements are not the same in a given symphony, why call the whole symphony in that key? Is it merely for convenience? Do we really mean that the Fifth Symphony is the Symphony in C minor, A flat major, C minor and C major? That is a long title to use.

Let us examine for an instant the first movement of the Fifth Symphony. After we have played a few phrases we find that we are no longer in minor at all and have passed to the key of E flat major. The first movement then is not all in the same key. If we are to expect change of key and mode in a single piece and still preserve an effect of unity, there must be some rules governing key selection and succession. There are, indeed, very definite rules and the relationship is called one of *tonality*. In every piece or group of pieces there is a central tonality, a key to be used as point of departure and conclusion. This must be kept always in view by repetition and emphasis; because it is so much more important to the piece or group of pieces than any key incidentally used, it gives its name to the whole work.

Before we go further let us be sure that we understand the difference between *key* and *mode*. We found in studying the scale that we base our modern music on two principal scales which we call the major and minor modes. These are in themselves survivals of many other scales used in antiquity and called modes. We found that by arrangement of whole and half steps we could reproduce either of these modes using any tone as tonic. The name of the scale then will show the *mode*, major or minor and the *key* which takes its name from the tonic or fundamental tone. The sound of a mode is not changed by transposition to another key for the scale pattern remains unchanged. When we are told that a piece is written in D major, for instance, we know that it is based on the major scale with D as its tonic.

If the sound of scale does not change when produced in another key, why do we bother to shift keys in the course of a movement? Certainly the change from major to minor mode will give variety, but why change to another key that sounds just the same? The reason is that when a melody is in a given key, we always have a strong sense of the tone which is its fundamental. We think of all the other notes in relationship to that tone. When we change key, we begin relating the notes to a new tonic, a new tonal allegiance is established and this gives a feeling of variety and progress useful to sustain interest in an extended design. When eventually we come back to our original key, there is an unconscious recognition of our return and a consequent contribution to the sense of unity of the whole work.

Change of key is called *modulation*. There are laws of harmony governing modulation so that it is possible to change from any one of the twelve keys, major or minor mode, to any one of the others. These laws are based upon the discovery that every triad, with the exception of the one formed on the seventh degree of the major scale, leads a double life. The triad GBD, for instance, is the tonic triad of the scale of G but also the dominant triad of the scale of C. It also plays the rôle of sub-dominant triad in the scale of D, and even makes appearances in some of the minor keys. It is easy to understand that this chord may serve as a basis for passing from one key to another, considered as a triad first of one key and then of another.

However, there is a simpler method of modulation which concerns melody, and which is much easier for the listener to perceive. Suppose we try a simple experiment on the piano. Do you recall *The Blue Bells of Scotland* which begins "Oh where and Oh where is your Highland laddie gone?" Try playing it on the piano in the key of C starting on G. You will find it is in four phrases arranged as follows: AABA. Did you notice as you used only the white notes of the scale of C that there was one false note on the piano, the one next to the last in the third phrase? Try using F sharp for this note. This seems correct. But F sharp is not in the scale of C and it certainly cannot be considered as a mere ornament for it sounds very important and leads the melody firmly up to G. What happens is that the F sharp belongs to the key of G and that when the G arrives it is actually the key note of the scale we are in. The F sharp has brought about modulation and changed the key. The change is only temporary. A moment later we feel that G is again being used as the fifth note of C.

Try the effect of deliberately leaving out the F sharp and playing the F natural so that the modulation does not occur. Aside from the fact that you are used to the other version, don't you find that you prefer the freshness which the temporary modulation brings about?

We sometimes have modulation in the very first phrase of a melody. If you will try to pick out *The Star Spangled Banner* in C using only white notes and starting on G you will run off the track on the second syllable of "Early" and will need the F sharp several times in the course of the melody. There are three short modulations to the key of the dominant in the song. The key of C, however, is reëstablished immediately in each case.

A good example of modulation is to be found in the *Minuet* from *Don Juan* by Mozart. This is in the key of F major. The second phrase commences with a B natural which is not in the scale, and which brings about a modulation to the key of C major. This new key is established at the end of the phrase with an authentic cadence in the accompanying harmony. The third phrase returns to the key of F major and the fourth concludes with an authentic cadence on the tonic. The pause in the key of C major, which has the dominant relationship to F major, constitutes a division of the minuet into two sections, each of which is usually repeated separately.

We can see, therefore, that the introduction of a note foreign to our key and its scale can bring about modulation. But this is not always the case. Sometimes the foreign note is obviously an ornament designed to lead back immediately to a degree of our scale. If you play the chorus of *Sailing, Sailing Over the Bounding Main* you will have to use, if you start on G, a foreign G sharp on the second syllable of "Over." Notice though that the note before it and after it is A and that it has no emphasis in the melody. It cannot affect our key at all.

Some of the melodies which we discussed in the chapter on Melody employ foreign degrees without modulation necessarily occurring. The *Habanera* from *Carmen* which goes down the chromatic scale does not modulate. *The Evening Star* modulates but it would be in difficulty if it had to find a diatonic scale for each note that it uses. This use of foreign degrees without modulation may be described as the influence of the chromatic scale upon otherwise diatonic melodies. In the case of a chromatic melody we turn to the harmony to see whether or not modulation has occurred.

Modulation in a folk song is almost always temporary. To remain long away from the principal key in a short piece of music would be to endanger its feeling of unity. When we study works which are long enough to be divided into sections, we find that a foreign key may be safely maintained for an entire section. We have already had a partial example of this in our analysis of *Humoresque*. The first and third sections are in G flat major and the middle part is in F sharp minor. This is not really much of a change because on the piano G flat and F sharp are the same. The only difference between the sections is a change of mode from major to minor; entire modulation does not occur.

There is a real change of key between sections of the Beethoven *Adagio Cantabile* which we examined in the last chapter. The odd-numbered sections are all in A flat major, but section two modulates to F minor and then E flat major. Section four is first in A flat minor and then in E major. These modulations have much to do with the feeling of variety and logical arrangement which we discovered in the composition.

We shall study several forms which are based upon the principle of key change as a fundamental part of their design; in these the key relationship of the several sections is usually tonic-dominant or in the case of the minor mode, tonic-relative major. Other more distant modulations occur in the course of works of some length but their relationship to the central tonality must always be apparent. In general keys may be regarded as neighbors when they have one note of their tonic triads in common. The great musical architects Beethoven and Brahms sometimes go very far afield in modulation, but there is always a logic about their progression away from and back to the *central tonality*.

What governs the selection of the central tonality of a composition? Are the keys different in sound so that they may be said to have characteristics? Franck had a great love for F sharp major, so much so that he always tried to reach this key when he had anything particularly beautiful to say. Musical comedy writers have a fondness for E flat major. Many people think that C major gives a rather bald effect, but that D major is a brilliant key. Many traditions exist as to the personalities of the different keys. Is there any scientific explanation of difference?

To begin with there is the question of notation. This involves a problem for the eye rather than the ear. C major uses no sharps and flats. G uses one sharp and F one flat. These are the easiest keys to read. The key of F sharp major requires six sharps or one more than we have black notes. This makes things very difficult for we have to turn a white note into a sharp and to regard F as E sharp. D flat requires five flats. Naturally these keys seem remote and difficult to the person who has to read all the sharps or flats. Possibly this may account somewhat for his attitude toward them. Also before equal tuning was used on keyboard instruments, these keys were unheard of. Possibly their comparative novelty makes them seem particularly interesting. At any rate there does not seem to be any real reason why any key should sound better than any other on the piano. As we move upward by key so that the music lies higher we shall naturally find an increase of brilliance, and vice versa when we move downward.

There is a good rejoinder to be made to the musician who insists that C and C sharp are entirely different in character of sound. In the first place the piano may be tuned below concert pitch, a phenomenon which often occurs, especially if the strings are rusty. Unless a musician has absolute pitch he will not be aware of this. The piano may be actually half a tone lower than standard so that what would be C sharp becomes C and C will become B. Actually the history of standard pitch shows us that since Beethoven's day, concert pitch has risen a half tone. If you want to play the exact tones that Beethoven imagined you will have to transpose down half a tone. The first movement of the *Moonlight Sonata* will not be in the supposedly poetic key of C sharp minor, but in the dull and pedestrian C minor. Our imagination combined with their varying difficulties can accomplish wonders in ascribing characteristics to the different keys.

In the case of the voice, key selection is very important because of its bearing upon range. The voice generally likes to have the tonic note in a central range so that the fifth will be in a high, powerful range above and the fifth below though not too low. Therefore in songs we often find versions in various keys to suit the different ranges of singers. This sometimes plays havoc with the accompaniment which, when moved down too low, will growl, and moved too high will lack force. In the case of choral music, a key note must be selected which will not take the basses too low and yet will be low enough to give authority to cadences on the tonic. Choruses, like pianists, prefer to read music which has a minimum of flats and sharps.

When we come to the violin family, we find choice of key much more important and for a very definite reason. The violin has four strings which are tuned G D A E, each a fifth above the other. When these notes are called for in the music, the violinist does not have to depress the string, but plays what we call the *open string*. This is not only easy to achieve but the tone has a slightly more open sound. As a result, when music is written in keys which use these open strings in their fundamental triads, the effect is more brilliant. The key of D which has an open string for its tonic, dominant and subdominant has always been a favorite tonality for violin pieces.

In the time of Beethoven and before, brass instruments such as the horn and trumpet could play only the harmonics of a given fundamental tone. Intervening degrees of the scale could be achieved by stopping the bell of the instrument with the hand, but this interfered with the volume of the tone as well as altering the pitch. In order to make instruments which could play the important notes of various keys, it was found necessary to make several instruments of the same type, each based upon a different fundamental tone. If the piece to be played was in E, an instrument based on E was used which could play the necessary notes. Naturally the horn and trumpet were as limited in melodies as our contemporary bugle, which still plays only the harmonics. During the nineteenth century, valves were introduced which altered the fundamental tone by shortening or lengthening the tube through which the air passed. These valves made it possible to play all the notes of the instrument's range. Today only two horns are used, the one in F and the one in B flat. The natural harmonics of each of these instruments are slightly better than the artificial tones produced by valves but not sufficiently so to influence choice of key of a composition.

The clarinet is made in two keys, one in B flat and one in

A. These instruments vary considerably. Both are superior
to the clarinet which was sometimes found in C. The B flat
clarinet is much brighter in tone than the A clarinet, although the latter is sometimes preferable for soft, mellow
passages. Usually when the key is a sharp key, the A clarinet
is used; when the signature has one or more flats, the B flat.
The clarinet in E flat, which produces a harsh, penetrating
tone, is sometimes found in the orchestra and often in the
military band.

These technical matters, which certainly have a bearing
upon the practicality of a key, may be responsible for our
idea of the personalities of keys; there is no other reason for
our distinguishing between them. When, however, we consider keys in succession, there is a very definite distinction
between them. When we modulate away from a key we go
in either one of two directions, either to the dominant which
is the fifth above or to the sub-dominant which is the fifth
below. If we start with C we find that modulating from
dominant to dominant through the keys of G D A E, we are
moving upwards and adding an extra sharp with each modulation. When we move in the opposite direction we move
downwards to the sub-dominant through F, B flat, E flat and
so on, each time adding another flat to our signature. Although it is possible for a composer to modulate without
moving through each neighboring key, he usually moves in
a given direction, toward the sharps with upward effect or
toward the flats with downward effect. We shall see, when
we come to examine processions of keys in the symphony
and in the opera, that the upward motion often gives a feel-

CYCLE OF TONALITIES

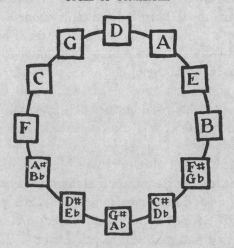

Key of C no sharps or flats

Key	Sharps	Key	Flats
G	1 (F)	F	1 (B)
D	2 (F,C)	B flat	2 (B,E)
A	3 (F,C,G)	E "	3 (B,E,A)
E	4 (F,C,G,D)	A "	4 (B,E,A,D)
B	5 (F,C,G,D,A)	D "	5 (B,E,A,D,G)
F sharp	6 (F,C,G,D,A,E)	G "	6 (B,E,A,D,G,C)
C "	7 (F,C,G,D,A,E,B)	C "	7 (B,E,A,D,G,C,F)

On the piano the keys of G flat and F sharp are the same by enharmonic relationship.

On the piano the keys of D flat and C sharp are the same by enharmonic relationship.

On the piano the keys of C flat and B are the same by enharmonic relationship.

ing of added strength and clarity, and the downward tendency increases the feeling of gloom. This resource of tonality legitimately contributes to the dramatic effect of music. Beethoven and Wagner, whose conception of music is essentially dramatic, make great use of it.

Wagner and his great predecessor in the opera, Gluck, also make use of tonality for dramatic effect by establishing keys in connection with certain moods of the drama. Although there is probably nothing inherent in the key to contribute to dramatic feeling, when we have heard keys associated with moods for a single act, we find that they serve to establish such a mood in our minds during the later portions of the work. The *Nibelungen Ring,* Wagner's cycle of operas, has a great advantage in this respect for he is able to start his key association early in the work and draw upon it for subsequent color. Certain keys he designates as heroic, certain others as base, tender, etc.

Our present age is a very interesting one from the point of view of composition. Although few critics will admit that much of what has been written in this century will survive or even improve upon closer acquaintance, composers are experimenting with the materials of music in every direction. Some of the discoveries already made have been great contributions to the resources of the composer's art. One experiment already embodied in many works, but chiefly to be found in the music of the Austrian composer, Schoenberg, deals with tonality. Schoenberg considers that the traditional idea of tonal relationships is somewhat limiting to the free development of music. For the customary diatonic scale with its irregularity of design, he substitutes the chromatic scale of equal temperament. Inasmuch as this scale consists of twelve semitones each equidistant from the other, the degrees have no tonal functions such as tonic, dominant and sub-dominant, and modulation is as impossible as the establishment of tonality. Chord combination instead of being made upon accepted principles is purely a matter of agreeable or disagreeable sound. Chord succession is not a matter of traditional laws but the individual taste of the composer.

At first glance, such a scrapping of musical logic would seem to result in loss of unity and subsequent chaos, and indeed to many ears such is the effect. Schoenberg, however, has a perfectly orthodox regard for unity and variety as the basis of design. He renounces the unity of tonality, but by repetition of subject matter and phrase arrangement, he preserves a feeling of unity which is clear once we have become accustomed to his strange sounds. The question is whether, in sacrificing tonality, he has secured sufficient freedom to compensate for the loss. This is a matter of taste. Many modern composers feel that it is now possible to relax the principles of tonality allowing for freedom and yet preserve an essential solidity beneath. Each of the so-called modernist composers seems to have his own particular feeling for this matter, but the tendency on the whole appears to be that Schoenberg has gone too far, and that steps must be retraced if music is to be clear and orderly. The principle which Schoenberg's music embodies is called *atonality* or *chromaticism*.

All through the nineteenth century, tonality has been in a state of expansion; more and more foreign notes have been admitted into harmonies and melodies but, until recently, no one has dared to advocate its entire abolition. Philosophically it all boils down to the same problem as that of every anarchy. How can you rebel unless you allow for the existence of some power as the object of your attack? Once we set up our own governments, we become the conservatives instead of the dashing young revolutionaries.

How can we train ourselves to perceive the arrangement of tonality of a work as it progresses? Without absolute pitch to help us the feat seems insuperably difficult. Also when we consider that the composer is bending every effort to make his modulations so smooth that we shall not feel a break in the normal flow of the music, why should we attempt to defeat his purpose? The answer is that save for understanding the structure of a work we choose to analyse closely, we need not concern ourselves much with tonality. Almost all music which is sufficiently well made to survive until it has reached our ears is well constructed tonally. When the arrangement of tonality of a long work is good, we have an instinctive sense of balanced structure; when a piece seems insufferably long, it may be that there is a fault of tonality somewhere. However, this is one aspect of music which we can enjoy without seeking to recognize. The musician must naturally pay attention to it, though often even he will not appreciate tonal subtleties until he is thoroughly familiar with the music. For us it is sufficient to realize that tonal relationships exist and form an important part of every musical design.

CHAPTER IX

Musical Subject Matter

IN our study of design we found that the elements of musical arrangement, rhythm, melody, and harmony were put together to make phrases; that groups of phrases were arranged in sections; and these so distributed as to make patterns both symmetrical and varied. We have also seen how tonality may assist in achieving variety of sound without destroying the feeling of unity. Simple music is readily put together in this fashion. It is possible to make a respectable composition by selecting two melodies of sufficient contrast, putting the second one in the key of the dominant or the relative, joining them with proper modulations, and repeating the first one for a conclusion. If further subtlety of design is desired, a few phrases based upon any of the material from the first or second melody may be added as a conclusion. Also a few introductory chords at the beginning would contribute to the impressiveness of the whole.

This is the formula for the composition of *potpourris* of airs, operatic or otherwise. Several melodies are linked together to make a perfectly understandable composition. You will notice that the final cadences of the constituent airs are sometimes modified in the interest of unity. This is disturbing, but often necessary if the piece is not to come to a dead stop in the middle. Perhaps you have heard in some medley of American airs, *Old Black Joe* taper off into another melody without ending at all. The last song to appear is naturally given the privilege of coming to a full cadence, but the others are apt to suffer alteration.

With very little skill at the piano, you can make your own medleys of favorite airs. You might, if you can play, try this for a medley; strike three authoritative chords using the notes GBD (the dominant triad of C major which is to be our tonality) dispersed as your fingers desire for an introduction, then plunge into *Old Black Joe* in the key of C. At the end of this, unless you have had experience, do not try to interfere with the final cadence, but begin right away with *Way Down Upon the Swanee River* in G. You won't absolutely need a modulation, for the key of G is so close that the joint will not be too awkward. At the end of this, go back to *Old Black Joe* and the key of C. For a conclusion it would not be too difficult to repeat the music for the words "I'm comin'." Do this twice and play the second one more softly than the first. Then end by two chords of C with C in the bass and C on top. You will be the author of a simple paraphrase which you could call "Stephen Foster Reverie" or something else that might suit your fancy.

Now there would be much to criticise in the design of such an arrangement. The chief fault is that the conclusive cadence of the first part rather defeats our wish to prolong the line further. Also, near though it is, our modulation seems rather abrupt. Also our repetition of first section by the third is a bit literal. But even if we were to correct these faults, would the composition be entirely satisfactory? No; because these two songs are musical entities in themselves; they were not designed to go together, and any alteration of their melodies which will make them fit better, will tend to destroy the original beauty which they contain.

This explains why the potpourri is at best an unsatisfactory form. If its unity is good enough to give us a well-balanced design, we generally find that some of its melodies have been fatally tampered with. It is like listening to a wandering speech in which the speaker forgets what he is talking about and deals with many irrelevant subjects. If he is very diffuse he must compensate for his mal-arrangement of ideas by charm, wit, delivery and so on. As in a speech, we like a reasonable amount of concentration in music. If several sections go to make up a composition, we want to feel their logical relationship. This can only come from their having been conceived in the mind of the composer to succeed one another.

As a matter of fact there is often a central unity of idea in a long work which is just as noticeable as the unity of tonality. This is the subject matter of the composition. It must be of sufficient interest to attract our notice and must be clearly stated at or near the beginning of the work. It is particularly important to concentrate on the first notes of a piece to which we are listening, for these generally contain the principal subject matter of the entire composition. Other ideas may be introduced later, but they are subsidiary and usually somewhat fragmentary, so that they will appear in proper relationship to the central subject. The central subject will dominate the design, will be heard most frequently and will usually be the most interesting.

This subject may not be a whole melody; it may consist of only two or three notes sufficiently arresting in their arrangement to imprint themselves upon our memory. Suppose we play a very familiar and popular piano piece, the C sharp minor *Prelude* of Rachmaninoff that we discussed in the first chapter. It is readily divisible into three sections, the third like the first, but so arranged in disposition on the keyboard as to sound more impressive. The middle part is different, but is in the same key as the other sections.

Do you notice that the three heavily accented notes which begin the piece are heard many times in the course of sections one and three? True, they are not usually the same tones but their rhythmic pattern is unvaried. This pattern is stated so often and so authoritatively that after we have heard the piece a number of times, we readily accept these notes as the central subject. Once we have recognized them as such, we get pleasure in observing how they move about the scale. This tonal variety might be considered as a ramification of the central idea.

If you look closely at the middle section, unmistakable because of its increased motion, you will see that the four notes which are on the top of successive arpeggios also provide a descending figure, this one closely spaced and based upon the chromatic scale, but not very far afield from the first subject. This second part of the *Prelude* could not serve as a piece by itself; the idea is not so arresting as the first one, the section does not seem complete. It is satisfactory as a dependent section, adding variety to the whole design.

Here finally we discover something concrete as to what this piece is about. It may represent grief, anger, yearning, horror or anything you wish, it can also serve as the embodiment of a story if you care to imagine one, but we can all agree that musically it is about a descending melodic figure of three notes of equal value. As a matter of fact, it is said that Rachmaninoff undertook the work as a study to see what he could do with such a simple figure.

Let us turn to a much longer and more important work, one which you probably have heard, the first movement of the C minor, the Fifth Symphony of Beethoven. This is a piece which will consume a number of minutes and more than one side of a phonograph record. Since it is in the complex sonata-form which we have not yet studied, we shall probably lose our way and find it difficult to follow. There will be a number of themes and several sections. Suppose we try it and see if we can find our way about at all. The first thing we hear is a group of four notes arranged in this rhythm. The first three constitute an anacrusis to the accented beat of the fourth. The melodic curve is downward, the first three notes are the same, the fourth is a third lower. Before going any further let us make sure that this rhythm is impressed upon our minds. Tap it and sing the melody. Do you notice that it has a somewhat peremptory sound? Beethoven spoke of Fate knocking at the door. Let us not think of Fate though, but merely of these notes in their rhythmical grouping.

Are you ready to go on? Begin again and notice what happens next, a similar group beginning one note lower in the scale. As we proceed, the music is faster and more difficult to analyse, but if we listen carefully we discover that the

rhythmic idea which we first heard is still going on in one
form or another. And so on through this whole movement
this group of four notes seems to be dominating every section and every melody. Sometimes it is in the accompaniment, sometimes in the melody itself. Here indeed is unity
of idea. Even more than Rachmaninoff, Beethoven has succeeded in dominating a composition by a single idea and in a
piece several times as long.

Such a work is at the opposite pole from our *Medley of
American Airs*. It is just as varied, gives us very little literal
repetition but is all based upon a central idea. What a triumph of unity and variety! We shall find that few compositions are quite so closely knit as the Beethoven or even the
Rachmaninoff. These are unusual, but they prove what can
be done with a single idea in an extended work.

If we return for a moment to the folk song, we can see
that these simple melodies are often based upon a short musical subject which is contained many times within them. An
obvious example of this is *America*. Do you recall that in our
analysis we found that there was no literal repetition in this,
but that unity was obtained by the persistence of a rhythmic
idea? This idea, stated in the first measure, is the central subject of *America*. In *The Londonderry Air* not only is the
rhythm of each phrase exactly alike, but each phrase contains two statements of it. There is a slight variation only in
the second half of the fourth phrase. We have no trouble
then in deciding what *The Londonderry Air* is about.

The short central idea which forms the basis of a melody,
a section or a whole composition we call a *motive*, meaning
a concentrated musical subject. This idea may have all the

elements, melody, rhythm and harmony, it may consist of only melody and rhythm or it may be almost entirely rhythm. In general rhythm is the most characteristic element of a motive as in *America,* but in the motive of *Träumerei,* the melodic figure which begins each phrase is almost more important than the rhythm, so that we might call this a melodic

BONDAGE

FATE CHORDS AND BONDAGE FROM THE *Ring*

idea. In the case of certain motives of Wagner, harmony is the characteristic element. Such groups of notes as the *Fate* chords or *Bondage* from the *Ring* are chiefly recognizable by their harmony. It is difficult to separate the elements of music in describing motives. They may be presented without harmony, but rhythm and melody must necessarily co-exist.

The degree of concentration in a melody or in a composition varies enormously. Some melodies seem almost without central motive and some pieces are very loosely constructed. In general there are two types of composition: simple *me-*

lodic combination and *symphonic* structure. The greater concentration and interdependence of themes the composition contains, the more symphonic is its style. Symphonic music necessarily imposes greater demands upon the listener. It depends somewhat less upon successions of agreeable sounds than upon their logical relationship. Therefore, when our experience is limited and our understanding untrained, we quite naturally prefer the music which makes fewer intellectual demands upon us. But even in a relatively simple piece we have seen there exist certain symphonic relationships which, when we understand them, in no way interfere with our enjoyment. In the case of works more purely symphonic, once we have understood the logic of their construction, much is clear that formerly disturbed us, and the music is found to contain beauty hitherto unsuspected.

The subject matter of music may be stated in a *motive,* a *phrase,* a *theme* or a *melody.* We have seen that a motive is a single concentrated musical idea. A phrase, we know, is a musical sentence. It may contain more than one motive or several repetitions of a single motive. Melodies are built out of phrases. We seldom have a melody which consists of only one phrase. A melody may contain very little material which we could call a motive, but there generally is to be found some rhythmic idea or turn of phrase which appears more important than the rest of the material. A theme is nothing but a term for a melody used symphonically. It suggests that the melody is only a part of a larger work, and that it contains concentrated material suitable for musical development. Naturally in a theme, as in a melody, we find additional material besides its constituent motive or motives. This material serves as a setting or picture frame for the central idea. When we speak of a *thematic idea,* we are generally referring to the central motive of a theme.

The reason folk melodies do not make good themes, as a rule, is not only because they are always bringing forward untimely cadences, but because they seldom contain sufficiently concentrated material to suggest development. All the great composers, or at least most of them, have used folk tunes symphonically; but usually they alter them so that the melodies lend themselves more readily to symphonic uses. An interesting instance of the difficulty of developing such a melody is to be found in the last movement of the First Symphony of Brahms. After the poetic introduction with the famous horn call, the *allegro* commences with a melody which, although original with Brahms, has the character of a folk song. We notice that in the course of the movement it is repeated as a whole or in large part many times, but is not often broken up and developed because it contains no concentrated ideas. As a result, the composer is compelled to produce much additional material which will serve this purpose, and the movement becomes rather long. No one will say that Brahms has not made a masterpiece in this movement, but we can admiringly watch his struggles with a theme which is essentially unsymphonic.

If you compare the early operas of Richard Wagner with those produced in his maturity you will notice the change in thematic content. In such operas as *Lohengrin* and *Tannhäuser,* the themes are long and very melodic, lending themselves readily to repetition, but not much to change, whereas in the later works, the *Ring, Tristan* and *Parsifal,* they are short, concentrated motives which help to produce the symphonic aspect of the mature Wagnerian music drama.

Too much concentration is not desirable. Not every composer can make a few notes sufficiently striking as to be memorable. We like a degree of melody in our themes, for from melody comes the greatest beauty to be found in music. In some modern music we find motives which are well calculated to provide the intellectual content now so desired, but lacking in melodic appeal. Such motives often suggest mere figuration which is admirable when used for accompaniment to melody, but makes rather meagre fare when constituting the principal musical dish. To say that a composition is intellectually well constructed does not prove that it is something we want to hear or even that it is musical. Unless the melody which comes out of a motive has some appeal as melody, mere ingenuity of construction will not suffice.

Many composers use more than one motive in the principal theme, so that it becomes a multiple idea, one which contains its own contrasts. In this case the subsidiary themes which would ordinarily serve as contrasting material to develop in relationship with the central idea may be regarded as interludes or conclusions of sections. The best sort of contrast in music is between rhythmic vigor and melodic expressiveness, a sort of masculine and feminine relationship suggestive of incompatibility, agreement or capitulation. The principal themes of many symphonies are fashioned in this way. For example, examine the first theme of the first movement of Mozart's *Jupiter* Symphony in C major. First we have this vigorous rhythmic idea:

[musical notation]

It is succeeded immediately by an expressive melodic figure in this rhythm: *[musical notation]* Notice that the two motives are immediately restated in the key of the dominant, and after this come a lively phrase or two which look new at first but soon appear as expansions of the rhythmic idea just stated. Later on we shall recognize these two motives, sometimes together, sometimes considered separately, repeated literally or in a different guise.

The first theme of Beethoven's Sixth Symphony, the *Pastoral,* is particularly rich in contrasting ideas; when expanded these come to have great significance. Here is the rhythmic scheme of the first four bars:

[musical notation]

This apparently simple theme has no less than three motives. The first one is of both rhythmic and melodic importance:

[musical notation] Notice that the essence of the melody is that the first three notes rise and the last one descends a step. The next motive begins upon the last note of the former at the start of the second bar: *[musical notation]* This motive is pastoral in character. Beethoven repeats it many times, securing his variety by change of key. The third and fourth bars seem more vigorous as they develop. This is the

scheme: ♫ ♫♩ | ♩ If you proceed further, **you**
will find that the first theme is not yet complete. First we
have two repetitions of the first motive with two answers of
the second, the melody moving upward instead of down, and
then we have a new idea suggestive of a fragment of a hymn.
It starts at the beginning of the ninth bar; you will readily
recognize this rhythmic scheme:

$$\frac{2}{4}\ \ \ \ \downarrow\ \downarrow\ |\ \downarrow.\ \downarrow\!\!\!\flat\ |\ \downarrow\ \downarrow\ |\ \downarrow$$

From this point on you will find much repetition of these
ideas. If you play the whole movement you will hear some
other themes, but nothing so striking or important. Suppose
you familiarize yourself with these four motives and see what
luck you have in finding them throughout the movement.
You will be surprised how well you are prepared to enjoy
the whole movement, although it is even longer than the
first movement of the *Fate* Symphony.

Let us look at the subject matter of a Brahms symphony.
Even more than Beethoven, Brahms unifies the texture of
his works. They are great examples of musical logic as well
as sources of some of the loveliest melodies in the literature
of music. Suppose we examine the first theme of the Fourth
Symphony in E minor. You will find the first phrase very
long, eighteen bars in fact. It consists of several ideas, two
of which are used sufficiently to justify their being regarded
as motives. Let us look at the first eight bars which contain
the first motive. Here they are rhythmically:

[musical notation in 2/4 time]

There is not much significant about this rhythm. It consists, like the Dvořák *Humoresque,* of the repetition of a single fragment. What gives it character is the melodic disposition of the notes. This is one theme which you could recognize by its melody alone. What does it do? The notes seem related in pairs of long and short; notice that each second pair seems to complement the first. The first goes down and the second goes up. It is like a charming dialogue between two persons. As a setting for this there are arpeggios in the accompaniment. The first motive is built upon identical fragments of rhythm, but since it is melodic in character, we shall expect it to be repeated as a whole rather than in part.

The next four bars consist of four repetitions of this

rhythm: *[musical notation in 4/4 time]* This is more purely rhythmic in character, readily recognizable as a fragment, and we shall find it often so used. The other two rhythms make a nice

contrast, *[musical notation in 4/4 time]* in the thirteenth and

fourteenth bars, and in the fifteenth and sixteenth.

[musical notation in 4/4 time]

The next two bars form a conclusion on a suspensive cadence. All these elements thereafter are repeated with a new and more elaborate form of accompaniment.

Brahms does not feel that he has sufficient material here to sustain the whole work so he later introduces us to this rhythmic idea, one which has a very definite personality:

¾ ♩ ⁊ ♫ ♩♩♩ | ♩ˑ ♪♩ This symphony is

more complex than the *Pastoral* of Beethoven and you must not expect to follow it so well, but you might try playing over the whole movement and seeing how much of the subject matter you recognize.

We have gone far enough to realize now that themes have a tremendous influence in determining the character of a work. The personality of a short group of notes can lend its color to the entire length of a composition. See how those four notes which make up the motive of the Fifth Symphony of Beethoven make the whole piece sound ruthless and awful. The flow of the rhythms in the *Pastoral* Symphony gives it a sunny, outdoor quality. The melting, limpid melody which constitutes the first motive of the Brahms so softens the effect of the movement that he is compelled to stiffen its emotional fabric by bringing in later the vigorous rhythm noted above.

It is in musical subject matter or thematic content that genius reveals itself in great composers. Musicians can learn the art of putting tones into proper shape, although their talent for this naturally varies. These musical ideas, however, these germs of symphonic efflorescence are a matter of pure inspiration. Some composers are more melodically minded than others. Like Schubert, they seem to think in terms of melodies rather than in the short, succinct rhythmic fragments that lend themselves best to symphonic style. This does not mean that they are less great composers, it simply indicates that they are less suited to symphonic composition and do their best works in the shorter forms. Schubert, Chopin, Grieg, Schumann and Tschaikowsky are some of the great melodic writers of the nineteenth century. Beethoven, Brahms and Wagner are more symphonic.

It takes less effort to appreciate the works of the men gifted in shorter forms, therefore they are apt to be more popular. There is no reason why either group is to be considered greater than the other. If we appear as we go on to emphasize the symphonic group at the expense of the other, it is merely because it is somewhat more difficult to understand.

The duty of the listener toward musical subject matter should be clear. This is the vital essence of the whole art; it concerns the question of appreciation or mere unintelligent bystanding. Whether or not you recognize the form of a piece is relatively unimportant. It is very important that you know what a piece is about. If you will take the trouble to train your perceptive faculties in recognizing musical subject matter, you will appreciate forms by instinct. Anyone with as much knowledge of the elements of music as you already possess can train himself by listening to and identifying subject matter. The phonograph or the piano transcription of symphonies played by yourself are ideal, for you can stop or start at will. Make sure that you have thoroughly digested the thematic content before proceeding further in any extended piece. Learn to use musical terms to describe themes.

Don't rely upon such expressions as "wavy," "trill-like," "sad" or "dancey." You know what constitutes rhythm, melody and harmony. See how exactly you can describe the musical ideas which please you.

CHAPTER X

Polyphony

WE discovered that harmony could be regarded as a succession of chords or the simultaneous progression of combined melodies, and that accompaniments tended to be harmonic or contrapuntal in character. Early examples of harmony are almost entirely contrapuntal; the science of chord combination as distinct from counterpoint was not fully understood until the eighteenth century. We distinguish between *polyphony,* which is music of contrapuntal texture, and *homophony,* which consists of a single melody and chord accompaniment. During the latter half of the eighteenth century and all of the nineteenth the possibilities of expressive harmony were explored by successive composers to such an extent that counterpoint was relegated to a comparatively minor place in composition. The harmonic style is more dramatic, makes fewer demands upon the listener's attention and is more popular than the contrapuntal. However if we examine the music of the age of Palestrina, the music of Bach, or even of such figures of the nineteenth century as Beethoven and Brahms, we shall find that the polyphonic features of style outweigh in importance the purely harmonic ones.

The theory of counterpoint is based upon the assumption that the mind can assimilate and enjoy more than one melody at a time. This was the motivating principle of the great composers of the fifteenth and sixteenth centuries, Josquin des Près, Palestrina and Orlando di Lasso. The church was not entirely sure that such combination of melodies was suitable for religious services. Had it not been for the genius of these men in preserving a dignified style the while they were perfecting the contrapuntal art, it would have been banished from the service and the growth of music in Western civilization much retarded.

You may think that such a contrapuntal piece as a fugue of Bach is too complicated for your ears and that you prefer homophonic or single-melodied music. Are you sure? Let us take a very simple combination of melody that you may have seen attempted as a parlor trick. Play or invite someone to play for you Dvořák's *Humoresque* and sing at the same time *Way Down Upon the Swanee River*. You have probably been surprised and delighted with the effect. It is only possible to continue the combination for the first two phrases of the melodies because thereafter they suggest differing harmonies but you will observe that while it lasts your mind is perfectly competent to enjoy the mixed product while preserving the identity of each separate melody.

There is a popular glee club arrangement which combines three melodies. One group starts off with *Solomon Levi* and when well launched is joined by another set of voices intoning *The Spanish Cavalier*. Finally the trio is complete with the addition of *My Comrades,* a favorite college drinking song. The melodies remain distinct although forming an ingenious and harmonious combination. Of course it is easier to enjoy such counterpoint when the separate melodies are familiar, but you would not feel, if asked to listen to this example, that any outrageous intellectual demands were being made upon you.

There is another sort of counterpoint which is very familiar to you, the combination of melody found in the *round*. Even

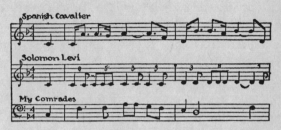

COMBINATION OF *Solomon Levi, The Spanish Cavalier* AND *My Comrades*

in beach picnic choral services where *Sweet Adeline* is the high point of the evening, *Three Blind Mice* or *Frère Jacques* often make their appearance. The round, as you will realize if you recall the effect, is a combination not of several melodies, but of one melody upon itself. This is achieved by starting each set of voices a phrase apart. When one set is singing phrase one, another is embarked upon phrase two, still another on phrase three and if there are enough performers another group upon the fourth. Each set of voices keeps going around and around; when the end of the last phrase is reached, the first one is freshly attacked. It is much easier to start a round than to finish it, for only one set of voices is ever at the end at one time. Usually fatigue or ennui cause the various entrants to drop out, leaving the survivors to finish alone. In order to achieve this familiar effect each phrase of the melody must be so constructed that it sounds well in combination with every other. Also the four voices are producing a four-note chord succession at the same time. This seems like a difficult feat for the composer to plan and achieve, and it is. Do you find the polyphonic combination agreeable? Does it impress you as being pure pedantry? Apparently if we are familiar enough with the elements going into these contrapuntal effects, they afford a pleasant and thoroughly understandable music.

There are two types of polyphony, the simultaneous statement of independent melodies and the doubling up of melodies upon themselves. The latter produces what are known as the contrapuntal forms, *canon* and *fugue*. The former is an accessory to other forms.

The first type we find more or less present in all music. Even the simplest composition usually contains a melodic bass. We have seen that the dividing line between counterpoint and harmony is very indefinite, that a hymn may be regarded as harmony or counterpoint. No accompanied melody is ever purely homophonic so long as there is a succession of chords. However, we can readily distinguish between degrees of polyphony in a work. When other melodies than the principal one impress themselves upon our consciousness, we realize that the composition is tending toward counterpoint rather than harmony.

But beyond the contrapuntal elements which may feature the accompaniment of a melody, composers sometimes, for the climax of a piece, combine important melodies which have been stated separately. One of the finest of such effects is to be found in the *Prelude* to *Die Meistersinger*. Three of the themes which are stated in the first part are combined in the climax; the first which forms the opening melody of the prelude serves as bass; in the middle appears the fanfare theme based upon simple chords, and above these the theme first introduced in E major, a broad melody destined to serve as part of the *Prize Song*. This combination is so ingeniously and spontaneously made that it may escape our notice at first. When we realize the neat trick which Wagner has turned,

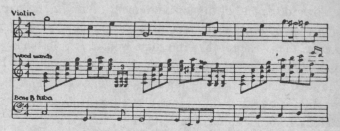

COMBINATION OF THEMES FROM *Die Meistersinger*

our delight in the composition is increased. If you want to try this on a record, you will find it in the second side fairly well along toward the end. You can recognize the place for there is a big crescendo which you think is going to lead to a great climax but which suddenly drops down to *piano*. This unexpected soft effect contains the combination of the three themes.

Brahms in the first movement of his symphonies sometimes combines themes in the long middle section which we call the development. In fact he combines his first and second themes in their initial statement in the first movement of his First Symphony. This is very unusual and rather difficult to recognize until you are very familiar with the work.

Franck is a great combiner of themes. You might almost say that he tests his themes for combination before he adopts them and always plans to put them together for the climax of the work. The organ choral in B minor contains an instance of one of the most successful of these combinations. The themes are each so individual and charming, it doesn't seem possible that they were planned to achieve this somewhat artificial relationship.

Toward the end of the last movement of the *Jupiter* Symphony of Mozart, there is a striking combination of four themes. This is probably the most remarkable instance of such combination to be found in all music, but it must be admitted that the four themes are somewhat lacking in personality, suggesting that Mozart sacrificed individuality of melody in order to achieve a striking effect. These are the rhythms of the four themes as they appear in combination:

The purely polyphonic forms mentioned above, canon and fugue, somewhat resemble the round. The canon is the older of the two. Early in the development of contrapuntal art, it was discovered that the combination of a melody upon itself produced an interesting effect. This combination was achieved in the same way as we have it in the round, that is when two voices are in canon, the second voice is a literal restatement of the first, separated by a short time interval. This results in the melody being doubled up upon itself. Two parts of it are being heard simultaneously. The difference between the canon and the round is that the canon goes on indefinitely, not rounding the corner and repeating the same phrases over and over again. Also the time interval which separates the entrances of the two voices is not necessarily the same. In the case of the round the voices are always a phrase apart, the second voice enters when the first voice embarks upon the second phrase. In the canon, the interval is usually closer, the second voice entering when the first voice has completed only one or two measures.

In passing let us understand that while polyphony can be produced with voices, with a group of instruments or even with a single instrument like the piano or organ, it is always customary to refer to the constituent melodies as voices. It is just as well to imagine them as separate singers or groups of singers. This keeps their independent relationship clear. In the case of keyboard polyphony we do not always use the same finger or even the same hand for a single voice.

Another difference between canon and round is that while in the round the second voice must always sing exactly the same tones as the first, in the canon it can sing them an octave apart or even at the distance of a shorter interval like the fourth or fifth. These last two intervals will naturally put the second melody in a different key and will make for great difficulties which are sometimes very entertainingly surmounted by a composer like Bach.

When the possibilities of canonic imitation were first dis-

covered, composers seized upon the idea to explore all sorts
of abstruse relationships. They would find a melody which
would make a good canon if combined with itself at the
proper time and tone interval, and would send it to a friend
asking him to find out just what these two intervals were.
When we realize that they allowed for canon by *reverse motion,* that is the second voice combining by going backwards
rather than forwards, the old device known as "the crab";
canon by *augmentation* in which the second voice had double
the time value to each note as the first, or by *diminution*
where it had less; canon by *inversion* where upwards and
downwards motion in the scale was reversed, we can understand that the sport was a fairly intellectual one.

Entirely apart, however, from its use for the testing out of
musical ingenuity, the canon has survived as a very useful
form of musical development. We seldom find pieces written entirely in canon since the time of Bach, who delighted
in the form; but we do find canon used incidentally in many
compositions. It makes an excellent distribution of the two
voices in a duet. Once the hearer knows what is going on, he
readily comprehends the relationship and enjoys it.

Canonic relationship was second nature to Bach. His music
contains many instances of remarkably interesting canons
which continue through the entire length of a composition.
We shall find it naturally in shorter works. A good set of
pieces to study if you are interested is the series of fifteen two-
part inventions, which young pianists so often study to develop independence of hands. Number 2 in C minor and number 8 in F major are in strict canon throughout. Numbers
1, 3, 4 and 10 begin as canons, but do not maintain the rela-

tionship. Number 10 is especially interesting because the tone interval used is that of the fifth although it is transposed down two octaves.

If you incline to more modern music, you will find a remarkable canon at the beginning of the last movement of the violin sonata of Franck. The top voice of the piano is repeated in canon by the solo violin. This relationship is strictly maintained through all the phrases of the long introductory melody. Notice that this canon does not provide all the har-

CANON FROM F MAJOR INVENTION OF BACH

mony but is supported by accompanying chords on the piano.

Franck of all nineteenth-century composers seemed to think most naturally in terms of the canon. In the last few measures of the Symphony in D minor you will notice that he has used the effect of canon with his short principal motive. This motive is the first music heard in the piece. On it is based the first theme of the composition, which is first heard after the slow introduction. This motive is repeated many times during the course of the first movement so that it becomes quite familiar. When it blares forth in this canonic relationship at the end, you will see how brilliant an effect is obtained.

All composers, whether or not they care to write strict canons, often use canonic imitation. This is an imitation of one voice by another which may not be necessarily literal but which gives the effect of canon. It is one of the most useful devices of musical development.

The fugue is really a product of canonic imitation. Unlike the canon however it is characterized by a great concentration of subject matter. Every fugue is built upon a short motive which is stated at the beginning of the work by a single voice. This motive is known as the *subject* of the fugue. A fugue subject, as in the case of a symphonic motive, determines the character of the whole composition. It is especially influential because the degree of concentration is much greater, and in the ordinary fugue there is only one subject. If you wish to study musical subject matter further, you could not find a happier field for exploration than the subjects of the forty-eight fugues in the two volumes of the *Well-Tempered Clavichord* of Bach. It is perhaps the greatest example of fertility of ideas in the literature of music. Each fugue subject contains the whole essence of a composition; it is individual, colorful and concentrated in the space of a few measures.

When the subject of the fugue has been stated, a second voice enters in canon on the fifth, that is the second voice repeats the subject literally in the key of the dominant. This repetition of the subject in the dominant is known as the *answer* to the subject. While the second voice is stating the answer the first one takes up new material which we call the *counter-subject* if it develops any thematic significance in the course of the piece. Often it is merely counterpoint of no especial interest and will not be repeated, but again it can develop an importance second only to the subject. Here canonic relationship ends; the two voices are free to proceed as they wish in counterpoint. Shortly thereafter a third voice will enter with the subject to be followed by a fourth voice stating the answer. The two original voices meanwhile are proceeding in counterpoint.

Fugues may be written for any number of voices from two to eight. After the subject and answer have been stated in turn by each of the voices, there follows a short free section to be followed by further entrances of the subject and answer. You will notice that no matter how many voices there are in the fugue, an entering voice always states either the subject or the answer. When voices temporarily drop out at the direction of rests, they almost always make their entrance again with the subject. During the course of a fugue one or another voice is usually to be found singing the subject or answer. You may not at first notice this because entrances in inner voices are so easily hidden by the counterpoint above or below them. If, however, you concentrate upon the initial statement of the subject and listen attentively as the composition proceeds, you will hear it woven in and out of the texture of the music. This makes the fugue a very entertaining sort of musical pattern. In the first place you have only to recognize one musical idea because the counter-subject is not often of great importance. Then you will find that this idea does not change but is tossed about from voice to voice, making frequent appearances.

When the fugue subject is not being stated by any one of the voices, we call the material *episodic*. Episodes are usually designed to bring about further statements of subject or answer. The plan of the fugue is a simple one. It is put together by a system of related keys. The first part states the subject and answer in each of the constituent voices. Thereafter the subject appears in various designated keys, separated by episodes. Eventually the original key reappears and the fugue is brought to an end.

There are certain devices which are sometimes found in fugues to vary this simple scheme. One of these consists of overlapping statements of the subject by several voices. This is called *stretto*. It is somewhat like a traffic jam. Instead of the voices stating the subject in orderly procession, several of them rush in at once so that while they are not singing together in unison, they are engaged in singing different parts of the subject at the same time. When you have the subject well in mind, you will find the effect of the stretto very amusing. It generally comes, if present in the composition, just before the triumphant last entrances of the subject in the home key. Many examples of stretto, which occur throughout the composition, may be found in the *B flat minor fugue* from the first volume of the *Well-Tempered Clavichord*.

Two other devices, which are favorites of Bach, come from the intellectual pursuits of the early experimenters in canonic relationship. These are *augmentation* and *diminution*. While one voice is stating the subject, another may be engaged in stating it with time values twice as long or twice as short to serve as counterpoint. Not many fugues are constructed with these complicated devices. If you wish to study one which contains some of them, examine the *E flat minor fugue* in the first volume of the *Well-Tempered Clavichord*. This one makes use of augmentation and inversion of the subject in stretto with the original version.

There is also what is known as the *double fugue,* one containing two subjects. These subjects may be stated simultaneously at the beginning and developed together, or the second one may make its appearance after a number of statements of the first subject.

In general, however, the fugue is a simple pattern based upon a single idea. The only reason it is at all difficult to follow is that you may not be accustomed to listening to counterpoint. Once you realize that the object in listening is to recognize the single idea as it appears here and there in the contrapuntal web, and that the subject is always stated alone at the beginning of the work, you should find it comparatively easy. When you have heard a number of fugues, you will discover that they are varied and interesting. The little *G minor Organ Fugue* of Bach, for instance, is catchy and tuneful, whereas the *Great Organ Fugue in G minor* by the same composer is mighty and overwhelming. We find not only that the fugue is a form that appeals to us by its logic, but that listening to its unfolding may be an exciting experience.

Bach wrote many fugues. In his time the symphony did not exist and he chose the fugue as his principal instrumental form. You will discover that the fugues in the two volumes of the *Well-Tempered Clavichord* are shorter than the organ fugues but have a greater range of expression. Each one presents a distinct musical mood, ranging from sparkling gaiety, as in the *C sharp major fugue,* volume 1, to the expressive sadness of the one in *G sharp minor* from the same volume. The organ fugues, built for the greater sonority of the instrument, have as a rule longer and more impersonal subjects, and make less use of chromatic harmony. They often build up to impressive climaxes.

Near the close of his life, Bach summed up all the knowledge of a lifetime of composing in an impressive set of fugues based on a single subject, called the *Art of the Fugue*. For many years this collection was regarded as of purely theoretical interest, but with the recent popularity of all his music,

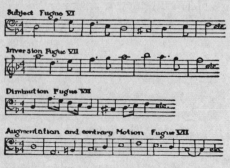

EXAMPLES FROM ART OF THE FUGUE BY BACH

it is now frequently played in concert and has been recorded in an arrangement for string quartet.

The fugue was developed from a scheme of imitation found in the sixteenth-century *motet* which in turn was suggested by the canon. It can be written for voices or instruments or both. Bach used it for his principal instrumental form and also made use of it in his choral works. Since his time not many instrumental fugues have been written by the great masters, but the fugue has remained active in choral music. In the oratorios and masses of Mozart, Beethoven, Mendelssohn and Brahms, you will find many fugues. Verdi even used a fugue for the choral finale of his opera *Falstaff*.

Choral fugues are easy to follow but do not always obey the rules strictly. They are regular enough to serve our purposes, however, for they present the essential idea of the fugue, that is the treatment of a single subject by the separate voices. Handel's *Messiah* has a number of choruses which are somewhat fugal in style, but there is one *And with His Stripes We Are Healed* which is a good example of a regular four-voice fugue. The subject is stated by the soprano which is followed by the alto singing the answer, the tenor the subject and the bass the answer. You will notice that occasionally the answer will vary a note or two of the subject. This is done to preserve the proper relationship of key between the subject and answer, but it generally has little effect on the character of the response and it need not concern us here. You will notice that in this fugue of Handel the counter-subject is quite important and is often repeated.

The *Mass in B minor,* Bach's choral masterpiece, contains a number of fugues. The first and second *Kyrie* are both in fairly strict form. The second is perhaps more regular than the first which has long episodes, but the subject of the first is so arrestingly beautiful that it is easy to follow. The first *Credo* is a majestic fugue made on the traditional tones of the Credo as used in the early church. In this you will discover that Bach has used the subject in augmentation in the bass about three-quarters of the way through the composition.

Your study of polyphony will help you to enjoy these great choral works. In general they are all constructed according to polyphonic principles, using the devices of canon, canonic imitation and fugue as the basis of voice writing. Occasionally a chorus will appear which is harmonic in style, but this, especially in Bach and Handel, is comparatively infrequent. The more we hear them the more we come to appreciate the rugged strength of the polyphonic style. It may impose greater demands upon our attention, but once understood it turns out to be a music of such rich and solid texture that our less difficult homophonic music seems rather pale beside it.

Before you go on to the symphony, you should examine some of the works of the great sixteenth-century masters like Palestrina. Here the polyphony is unaccompanied and consequently very clear. Some of the choruses will appear harmonic in style and some entirely contrapuntal. You will not find any examples of fugue, but there are many canonic features and effects which much resemble the fugue in style. This music, undramatic, somewhat unemotional, scorning pretty melodies and lush harmonies, presents an aspect of nobility and strength which is ideal for the religious service and for performance in great cathedrals. Church composers since the time of Palestrina have never succeeded in equalling the heights of pure spirituality which are to be found in his music. He is one of the great geniuses of all times.

Polyphony, relegated to a position of lesser importance than harmony, that new science which so fascinated the nineteenth century, has never died out completely nor can it ever. Today it is enjoying considerable vogue among the new composers. In their anxiety to cast off all the influences of the last century, they have found the contrapuntal art ideal to embody their principles. As a result Schoenberg, Stravinsky, Bartok and Hindemith and their imitators are continually striving after polyphonic combinations. Their free treatment of tonality and harmony has enabled them to write counterpoint which is not restricted by traditional ideas of agreeable sound. This is doubtless somewhat easier to do, but it is not necessarily wrong. As we have seen, our ideas of what constitutes agreeable sound are so changing and unpredictable that we must assume the contrapuntal combinations of these composers agreeable at least to their own ears. It remains for us to familiarize ourselves with the works, if we care to form an intelligent opinion, pro or con, about them.

It is well to sum up the case of the polyphonic versus the homophonic style at this point in our progress. Music is certainly a large enough art to contain them both. They may be advantageously combined in single compositions as Beethoven and Brahms have shown us. Still there are certain disadvantages about pure polyphony. It often produces a music which is opaque, containing too much diversion of melody, ambiguity of rhythm and insecurity of cadence. Homophonic music, moving simultaneously in a single rhythmic impulse, dominated by a single melody, is more dramatic and clearer. Often it is more efficient in purpose, just as a clever individual can accomplish more than a committee of talented persons. Separate melodies have separate interests which the best polyphony cannot always serve. The homophonic style brought a new eloquence into music which we should not discard, no matter how great our temporary irritation at the immediate past. A gifted modern composer, Prokofieff, has recognized the danger of assuming that our ears can appreciate many strands of melody when presented simultaneously. Two and sometimes three voices, he claims, can be heard simultaneously with understanding, but when we get to four, five and six, they become a muddled whole exceeding our powers of attention. Music is designed to be heard as a whole, not to be dissected for a school teacher's holiday.

One great advantage about the tendency today toward polyphony is that it lays emphasis upon melody rather than harmony. Composers who think only in terms of pretty chords cannot write polyphony. Melody must continue to be the horse and harmony the cart if the art is to progress. Another advantage about polyphony is that its tendency is to keep the voices moving forward rather than to slip into easy periodic cadences which fail to sustain the interest. It provides a rich texture beside which the most elaborate harmony is rather flat. The best argument in its favor is, however, that it is the medium selected by Johann Sebastian Bach, the greatest figure in the history of the art of music.

CHAPTER XI

Development

MENTION has already been made of the process called *development* in which symphonic themes, like ideas in an essay, expand and progress in logical manner. There are after all only three things a composer can do when he has stated a musical sentence. He can produce another idea for contrast and variety, he can repeat the first sentence for the sake of unity and clarity, or he can carry the thought of the first sentence forward by dealing with its subject matter in a new way. We have seen that it is possible to make very acceptable music by the use of only the first two resources. Exact repetition and contrasting material are the basis of many fine compositions. Music of the melodic type without great concentration of subject matter usually contains little development of material. Such music is to be enjoyed chiefly for its sensuous beauty.

Many people claim that the principal object of music is indeed sensuous beauty, that its essential nature is violated when it is forced to serve as a vehicle for thought—that is musical thought, the logical relationships of themes brought about by development. Such people are entirely justified in preferring melodic to symphonic music, Chopin to Brahms and Verdi to Beethoven. But it would be unfortunate if we were to prescribe only one sort of music for the composer to write, regardless of the nature of his talent, and only one for the listener to hear, not taking into account the individuality of his taste. As a rule people who have a genuine love for music also have a wide range of enjoyment. Mr. H. L. Mencken in reviewing a book, which he did not think worth the paper it was printed on, observed that he seldom failed to get pleasure out of a book, even a bad one, because he liked books. When so-called music lovers exhibit violent enthusiasm for one sort of music and violent prejudice against every other, one suspects them of snobbishness rather than of discriminating taste. The reader is urged to learn to enjoy as many kinds of music as possible. What appears distasteful often becomes a source of the greatest enjoyment when it is familiar enough to be understood. Allowing for natural differences among listeners in intellectual power and grasp, there has never been written a work of such proportions that the average mind cannot understand it. Also such simplicity and unpretentiousness as may be found in the work of any recognized composer or in any surviving popular music need not be scorned even by an Einstein.

In music of the melodic type we find a beauty analogous to that of lyric poetry. In music of the symphonic type, logical thought, such as characterizes a philosophical treatise or a great drama, is suggested. The music of the great musical architects, Bach, Haydn, Mozart, Beethoven, Brahms, Wagner, Franck and Strauss, is characterized by development of thematic ideas which is as important as the inspiration of the ideas themselves. In this development we find their technical skill, their ingenuity and their power of expression at its height.

The untrained listener generally approaches the great symphonic works with some misgivings. He finds that shorter, simpler compositions are easier to understand and that the long sustained symphonic movement exhausts his powers of attention. When the music continues indefinitely and we lose track of it, the mind wanders and the only effect produced is mystification or boredom, punctuated by the impression of an occasional climax or lyric phrase.

The best way to approach the problem of understanding symphonic music is to select one composition for study. Play it over a number of times until you begin to recognize and anticipate certain definite musical effects. Try then to isolate the thematic material and examine its rhythmic and melodic character. With the themes in mind, play over the composition again and try to sense the relationship of various passages to these themes. You will discover that all the music bears a logical relationship to them, providing repetition, variation or contrast. When you have cleared up all these relationships as well as you can, play the entire movement again without pause. You will discover that your attention no longer wanders and that you are probably having a very good time.

Once you have completely mastered one symphonic movement, you will find that, even at the first hearing, you will get more out of the next one you try. Remember that familiarity with a piece of symphonic music is the best key to understanding it, and, contrary to the experience that you may have had in the case of popular music, familiarity with such a composition will constantly increase your pleasure in hearing it.

Before you undertake such a study, it will be profitable to consider the nature of musical development and to examine some of the devices which are employed in the great symphonic literature. For an extended composition we must have concentrated musical ideas, development of these and formal organization. Until you have reached the point of understanding musical subject matter, little will be gained by the study of development. If you do not understand the matter under discussion, even the most logical arguments will fail to interest you. Similarly the formal organization is meaningless unless we have some appreciation of the elements which constitute the design. The forms of the symphony will be described in the chapters following. We shall now study symphonic texture, or development.

But we have not yet defined *development*. If it is not repetition and not contrasting material, it must be *varied repetition*. In even the simplest music we find some such variation. The suspensive and conclusive cadence changing an otherwise identical phrase in a folk song is a form of development. Such a song as *The Londonderry Air* or a piano piece like *Träumerei* where the melody is varied over a constant rhythm, is an example of more advanced musical development. Both these pieces are far removed from the simple reiteration of a single phrase found in savage music. As a rule, the longer a work is, the greater will be the need of varied repetition and the likelihood of our finding it.

The first and most common form of development is *repetition by transposition*. This can scarcely be called development at all for the only element changed is the one of tonality. We shall often find it in the case of a whole melodic phrase or some fragment thereof, not necessarily changing the key but mounting up or down the scale. Several such repetitions we call a *sequence*. A very simple example is contained in *America* at the beginning of the second phrase, "Land where my fathers died." Here we have a sequence of two repetitions of the same melody, first on G and then moving down to F. You will probably recall many such sequences. Symphonies, particularly those of Haydn and Mozart, are full of them. Grieg sometimes uses so many sequences that the effect becomes tiresome.

The second type of development is *variation of accompaniment* to the same melody. A very simple example of this is the third section of the Rachmaninoff *Prelude* which we have already studied. The duplication of the original melody in octaves and broadening of the accompaniment is an elementary type of development. Development of the central motive by transposition is found in the first and third sections. Songs frequently employ variation of accompaniment. A good example of this is to be found in *My Heart at thy Sweet Voice* from *Samson and Delilah* where elaborate variation of accompaniment occurs in the second verse. In the second movement of the *Sonata, Opus 13,* of Beethoven, which we have studied, the initial melody of eight measures is repeated four times during the course of the piece, using both transposition and variation of accompaniment. The third and fourth repetitions vary the rhythm of the accompaniment. Sometimes for the repetition of verses of folk songs variety is secured by variation of the harmony. This is a favorite device of such a composer as Grainger, who specializes in folk songs. *Shepherd's Hey* is a good example of this type of development.

The third type of development consists of the simple change of the melody or theme from major to minor or vice versa. A good example of this type is to be found in the second movement of the *Surprise* Symphony of Haydn. The initial melody which is in major in the first section appears later on in the minor mode. This type of development is usually characterized also by variation of accompaniment.

The fourth type of development consists of *melodic variation*. Such variation is obtained by (a) retaining the tones or tonal outline of the melody and changing its rhythm, or (b) keeping the same rhythm and changing the succession of tones.

An example of (a) is to be found in the *Andante Con Moto* from the Fifth Symphony of Beethoven. The initial theme heard on the violas and cellos later appears in two different rhythmic guises. The first change consists of the addition of notes to the melody so that the whole appears an even rhythm of sixteenth notes. The original notes of the melody appear in the new rhythmic framework, but the effect is quite different. The second change is to a more elaborate melody of thirty-second notes.

An example of (b) is *The Londonderry Air*. The third and fourth phrases of the melody have the same rhythm as the first two, but the notes of the melody are different. Another example is to be found in the repetitions of the principal motive from the first movement of the Fifth Symphony of Beethoven. This motive is first developed by transposition but later we shall find the same rhythm with notes in different relationship to one another, here moving upward instead, of downward and again using the interval of the fifth rather than that of the third.

A fifth scheme is *development by combination;* this somewhat resembles the second type, variation of accompaniment, but whereas in the former we are concerned with a change in accompanying harmony, in this case the music is necessarily polyphonic. It provides for the combination of an independent melody with one or more new melodies, thereby changing the musical effect of the original melody. An illustration of this type of development is found in the second movement of the Seventh Symphony of Beethoven. The rhythmic theme which begins the movement is combined at the twenty-seventh bar with a new expressive melody. Another example is the theme combination which occurs beginning at the forty-fourth bar in the Finale of the Third Symphony, the *Eroica*.

In our study of polyphony we came upon another variety of this species of development. We saw that themes originally stated alone could be combined as in the *Meistersinger* Prelude, the Franck Choral or the Brahms Symphony. This is a form of development and a very subtle one, for instead of giving additional emphasis to a theme by stating it in combination with a new one, it shows the relationship of one theme to another already heard, bringing about a fine unity between the two as well as added significance to both of them. Another example which you will discover when you become sufficiently familiar with the work, which is long and difficult to understand, is in *Till Eulenspiegel* of Strauss. There are two principal themes relating to Till which are in the process of development all through the work. There is one point near the climax where the two themes combine with delicious effect, first one and then the other on top. The first theme is stated almost at once by the horn; the second is the odd figure which soon thereafter skips about on a solo clarinet. *Till Eulenspiegel* is a very good piece to study to train yourself to follow development. The themes are individual, easily remembered and one or the other is almost always the basis for the music.

Polyphonic forms contribute another familiar device in development, one which we have already studied, *augmentation* or *diminution* of theme. We shall call this the sixth type. Taking a theme twice as slowly or twice as fast as we are accustomed to hearing it brings about a great change in its effect. It undoubtedly suggests aspects which we have not thought of. A fine example of augmentation is found in the treatment of the first theme in the first movement of the Fourth Symphony of Brahms. We have already examined this theme and seen how romantic a melody it is. About two-thirds through the first movement when we are led by the tonal and thematic arrangement to expect the theme to return in its original key, it comes back in augmentation. The effect is mysterious and impressive. Strauss, for another example, uses both augmentation and diminution in *Till Eulenspiegel* to serve one or another purpose of the accompanying story. Examples of augmentation and diminution are clearly presented in Fugues six and seven from Bach's *Art of the Fugue*. The *inversion* of the theme which you will observe in these fugues may be regarded as an example of melodic variation.

The seventh type of development uses the characteristic forms of polyphony, *fugue* and *canon*. A fugue, developing as it does a single idea by transposition and combination, serves as a concentrated presentation of a single idea often useful to complete realization of the import of a symphonic theme. In the symphony we rarely find entire fugues as complete forms. However they often appear as *fughettas* or short fugal passages in the course of the development. A good example of this is to be found in the second movement of the Seventh Symphony of Beethoven. The original theme of the movement is developed successively by polyphonic combination, melodic variation, variation of accompaniment, and later by a short fugal treatment.

Canon and canonic imitation are also very useful in the symphony. An example of this which has already been quoted, the canon which Franck uses with his principal motive at the end of the first movement of his D minor Symphony, will suffice to illustrate this point.

Our development schemes so far have been mainly concerned with variation of an entire theme or melody by several devices. However, you will recall that in our chapter on musical subject matter we found that themes often contained several short motives readily detachable from the theme proper and stated separately for purposes of development. Such a theme we found in the first movement of the *Pastoral* Symphony of Beethoven. When these short motives are thus detached and heard separately, developed by transposition, in sequence, or by any other form of variation already noted, the theme itself is serving as a central subject, the various implications of which are being discussed by the music. This *breaking up of themes into fragments,* the eighth type, is the most familiar device of symphonic development. In the symphonies of Haydn and Mozart you will find that this is the principal scheme and that the treatment of the fragments or separate motives by transposition and sequence is easily recognizable.

In the eighteenth century when the symphony was standardized, this process of development was called the *working-out* of themes. The first movement always contained an entire section devoted to working out the themes. This was called the *development-section*. The entire movement, we find, is divided into three parts: the first one states the themes, the second develops them and the third restates them. We can see that this is a modification of the usual ABA form of simple music. The principal difference is that the sections are longer, contain more than one theme and that the second section, instead of bringing forward contrasting material, discusses the material already stated. This form is, therefore, much more closely knit than ordinary song-form; it is necessary that it should be because of its much greater length.

In listening to the first movement of a symphony you may find it difficult unless you are under the direction of a skilled guide to find your way about from section to section. The part devoted to stating the themes is often long and complicated. In the classic symphony it was always customary to repeat this part so that before embarking upon the development of the themes, the hearer might have the privilege of listening twice to the material. Also in the classic symphony, that is, the symphony before Beethoven and including his first two, the first section usually ends with a full cadence readily recognizable. Later symphonies often suppress the repeat of the first section because of their great length. This has one disadvantage because the longer the work, the greater our need of familiarity with the themes.

Let us see if we can find our way about the first movement development of the G minor Symphony of Mozart, probably his most popular symphonic work. It is ideal for our purposes for the development is based entirely upon the first theme, a very melodious and simple idea. This theme is stated almost immediately at the end of the first measure of accompaniment. It contains several ideas, only two of which are to be regarded as motives. You will be able to tell the end of the theme, for at its conclusion there is a suspensive cadence on the dominant chord and the first phrase of it is repeated. For the moment do not go beyond this point, but play over again the first two phrases. You will notice that the second is a repetition of the first by transposition down one note in the scale. The first phrase contains our two principal motives upon which the development is based. The division between the two will be immediately apparent. Let us analyse these motives. They are, to begin with, exactly alike in rhythm. Their difference is one of melody. Here is the rhythmic scheme:

Now although the rhythm is identical, we should never be in danger of mixing them up because the melody is so different. The first one begins with a group of three notes on two adjacent degrees, and after two additional repetitions of these, skips up a sixth. This skip of the sixth is very agreeable melodically. It is like a graceful leap prepared for by several preliminary steps. Perhaps more than anything it gives the character of grace and charm to the movement. The second motive comes down the scale from the top note of the leap and at the end repeats the last note. Where in the first motive there is a skip up, in the second there is a repeated note. The two motives serve as excellent foils melodically one to the other while the rhythm is giving unity to the whole theme. Let us call the first motive X and the second Y. Be sure that you understand them before proceeding.

Now either begin at the development; or pass through the first section without attempting to remember the other themes for since they do not appear in the development a further analysis of the remainder of the first section is not necessary at present. It begins with two short chords followed by several soft sustained chords in the wood winds. In the middle of these suddenly appears the phrase of the theme containing our two motives X and Y in a new key. There is a sequence of two more repetitions of this phrase each time descending into a lower key. The effect is one of temporary dejection to our spirited little melody, something is happening to it. Suddenly it appears decisively in the lower voices and is immediately answered by the upper ones in another key. This effect is repeated. The second time, when the upper voices answer and get to Y, we embark upon a new plan. Y is now changed so that it contains both the downward scale and the skip of the sixth at the end. It has therefore the two most interesting features of the melody. This altered form of Y makes three appearances and is followed by two appearances of X with the skip of a sixth suppressed and the repeated note added. X is now much less interesting. Mozart evidently wishes to concentrate upon the two degrees of the melody at the beginning of X. This he does for the rest of the development. Sometimes they go up, but more often down. This little fragment is repeated again and again by transposition, inversion and combination until suddenly we find it serving as preparation for the skip of the sixth; our original key has arrived and we know that we are at the beginning of the third section of the movement.

Here is the simple scheme of the development:

XY
XY } descending by transposition
XY

XY in lower voices answered in upper by XY in transposition
Same repeated in new key
Y with skip of sixth added in transpositional sequence of three
X with skip of sixth suppressed in literal sequence of two
Development of X (first part by transposition, combination with new harmony and inversion of melodic fragment.

After several trials you will find that you can follow this scheme precisely so that at each instant you will know what is going on in the music. Naturally unless one is studying symphonic structure, such detailed analysis is unnecessary. The reason why such an analysis is undertaken here is to prove that each note in a symphonic work can be explained in its relation to the whole and to the central idea. What you should be able to do, in order to enjoy this symphonic movement intelligently, is to be able to recognize the themes. Certainly Mozart does not disguise these simple ideas beyond the point where they are easily identified as his simple scheme of development proceeds.

You will find that this is a typical working-out section of a classic symphony. None of them makes great demands upon our intelligence. Frequently they seem undertaken by the composer as a chore and add little to our musical pleasure. The developments of Schubert are often like this. He excels in beauty of theme and his themes always have melodic charm, but when he develops them, his interest and consequently ours is less great.

It is precisely in this matter of logical thought that Beethoven and after him Brahms appear so great. Beethoven seemed to feel that if a development section is to be undertaken, it should not be merely a display of the composer's ingenuity in variation and technical skill, but a system of logical thought rendered necessary by the nature of the themes themselves. Themes to Beethoven were not merely musical figures, but individuals with marked characteristics and fixed destinies. The first movement for him becomes a history of their relations with other themes of contrasting natures, a sort of magnificent battleground. Accordingly in Beethoven the symphonic form takes on the nature of a great drama where tremendous things happen, both tragic and sublime. Although we should guard against allowing our imaginations to confine the music in terms of actuality, we are missing the true import of the music unless we sense something of what is occurring to the thematic protagonists.

We should expect to find, if this dramatic import of his music is a correct interpretation, balance and symmetry of design yielding to continuous development to be indicated by succession of keys, growth or retardation of themes and increasing or decreasing sense of climax. This is precisely what we do find and what gives to the Beethoven symphonies their quality of sublime human utterance. In contradistinction to the classic symphony there is less symmetry between the first and third sections of the form. In Haydn and Mozart the third section is exactly like the first except for certain tonal relationships which we shall discuss later. In Beethoven the recapitulation of material in the third section always shows the mark of what has gone on in the development. Often this is suggested by so slight a detail that it escapes our notice, but it is always there. This is especially noticeable in a new type of development which we shall call *theme amplification,* the ninth type that we shall consider.

In the first movement of the symphony, which typical design is known as *sonata-form,* he sometimes alters themes by the change of a note or two of the melody and in this way revolutionizes their character. This change may occur in the development but it is more often indicated in the third or *recapitulation-section* where, so to speak, the casualty lists are summed up. The most obvious example of this method of treating a theme is to be found in the magnificent first theme of the *Eroica* Symphony, number three in his list of nine. This theme is based on the tonic chord of the key of E flat, the tonality of the symphony. When it is first stated it starts on the first degree and returns to it to pass to a weak ending upon a chromatic note not in the scale. When it is heard in the third section after it seems to have passed through one glorious victory after another, it is changed so that it ends by a triumphant affirmation of the fifth degree rather than a return to its point of departure.

Amplification of thematic material is, therefore, a device of development brought into the symphony by Beethoven although it did not originate with him, for we find eloquent examples of it in Bach's treatment of the choral. The choral

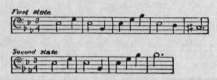

THEME FROM EROICA SYMPHONY BY BEETHOVEN

preludes of Bach, designed for performance by the organ during the service, are really variations upon the German church tunes. These variations are made according to many of the schemes which we have enumerated, but the most beautiful of all are the ones where, by theme amplification, he seems to irradiate the theme into a composition of unsurpassable loveliness. Perhaps the most beautiful example of all is the one on *O Mensch bewein dein Sünde gross* which is contained in the *Orgelbüchlein*. This melody is not to be lightly approached. Its beauty is of such spiritual depth that it can only be understood after long acquaintance. It is worth any effort necessary to capture it. Another example of this type is the choral prelude on *Wenn wir in höchsten Nöthen sein*.

It has been remarked that by changing the character of the symphony by the dramatization of themes and development, Beethoven took away from it some of its objective design. He used it as a vehicle to say something, not as a mere pattern of lovely sounds. In this way he was moving toward romanticism in music where the art took on a more expressive and subjective nature. It was not much of a step from this to program music and the attempt to deal with literal subjects as illustrated by the music of Liszt, Berlioz and Wagner.

The extravagant and overblown quality of later romantic music gradually demonstrated the folly of converting the art of pure sound into a language, which at its best could not fail to be less clear than speech. Today and for some years past composers have been rather penitent in their attitude about music as a language. Rather than claiming more for it, the tendency has been toward greater emphasis upon design and less preoccupation with emotional content. On the part of the leading European composers such as Stravinsky the reaction has been so violent as to deny to music any meaning beyond design. Beethoven, so long the monarch of all music, has suffered a loss of esteem; and the more objective music of Haydn is seen as the ideal embodiment of symphonic form. It is not necessary for us to take sides in the struggle at all. Theories about composition are best left to composers, and there is a suspicion in the mind of the public that if these gentlemen would concern themselves less with aesthetic platforms and manifestos, they might profitably devote their time to the composition of better music.

However, we cannot set back the clock and shut out the nineteenth century by acting as if it had never existed. There may be new formal discoveries available by examining the methods of the early masters, but the logical treatment of sonata-form by Beethoven will always appear as one of the greatest artistic achievements of the ages. Also we cannot deny to music its expressive content. Without this, music becomes a branch of higher mathematics, interesting to scientific musicians, but not to the world at large.

Beethoven's great successors, Wagner and Brahms, took entirely different features from his style to develop their own artistic personalities. Wagner was primarily interested in dramatic music and only secondarily in design. He sensed the quality of drama to be found in the earlier composer's symphonies and tried to transplant Beethoven's methods to the stage. The later operas of Wagner become long symphonies where certain Beethovenian tendencies are very apparent. Principally among them we find theme amplification as applied to development. In Wagner's case we have themes associated with characters whose histories are enacted for our benefit upon the stage. As the characters change so do the themes.

The principal theme of *Parsifal* which is stated at the beginning of the Prelude is usually associated with the idea of the communion service and the miracle of transubstantiation. In the drama of *Parsifal*, the communion service can only be conducted satisfactorily by one who is without sin. Parsifal proves eventually to be this rare sort of person. The basic theme, which rises in its first statement to a climax only to fall back rather unsatisfactorily, changes during the last act to an ending of triumphant affirmation, indicating in musical terms the successful conclusion of the drama. The theme used for the character of Parsifal likewise changes during the work from something rather tentative to a definite and heroic design.

Brahms as regarded by the romanticists was a reactionary.

He was very little interested in drama or musical story telling, and never even considered writing an opera. He was
primarily interested in musical design, not denying to music
expressive content as do many of the moderns, but allowing
this to be a part of his work without especial preoccupation
or plan. He did not renounce the symphony as conceived by
Beethoven; he simply accepted what features seemed best

THEME FROM *Parsifal* OF WAGNER

suited to his purposes and ignored the others. Therefore while
we find in Brahms a somewhat greater symmetry between
the first and third sections of sonata-form, and the usual persistence of themes in the recapitulation-section as originally
conceived, theme amplification becomes the principal plan
of his development-sections.

Instead of the development-section being a working-out
of material or a dramatic history of struggle between themes,
this part of the symphony becomes in Brahms the most lyric
of all. Themes which were beautiful as first stated become
almost unbearably lovely in development. Although he uses
in addition the familiar devices of combination, breaking up
into fragments and many other classic devices, it is this am-

plification of themes which makes his symphonies so eloquent. His one idea seems to be the production of lovely sound. Instead of accomplishing this in the manner of repetition and contrast which we find in Chopin, it is done by development and apotheosis of concentrated thematic material. Several examples of such amplification are noted below. The development of the Third Symphony is perhaps the most perfect from this point of view, so this is chosen for illustration.

In listening to a Brahms development, we shall have great need of familiarity with the themes. His use of rhythmic elements, his arrangement of phrase is often so subtle that we become confused. Perhaps it would be wiser to study Beethoven's method of development thoroughly before attempting Brahms.

One more method of development remains to be explained, the tenth or *theme disintegration*. It is found chiefly in the symphonic works of Beethoven where it plays an important part. Just as theme amplification suggests added power, theme disintegration is useful to indicate increasing weakness. By theme disintegration is not meant the separation of a compound theme into its separate motives as we find in Haydn and Mozart. It is rather the progressive disappearance of features of a single motive so that its musical character becomes weaker and weaker. In the Beethoven development there are generally two themes selected for combat. One of them usually grows while the other loses in force. This makes the dramatic implications of the movement very clear. Theme disintegration is so effective that one wonders why it is so seldom encountered in other composers.

THEME FROM BRAHMS' 3RD SYMPHONY

THEME FROM BRAHMS' 3RD SYMPHONY

THEME FROM BRAHMS' 3RD SYMPHONY

A very good example is to be found in the first movement
of the Fifth Symphony. We have already studied this movement as an illustration of theme unification. The starting
motive we discovered to be of such force that it dominated
and penetrated all the material of the movement. However,
there is a subsidiary theme used to unite the first theme with
the short lyric phrase constituting the second theme in E flat
major. This theme is a sort of horn call: it starts out with
the three short notes of the motive but instead of confining
itself to the one long note at the end characteristic of the
principal motive, it adds two others of great thematic importance. The melody of the three long notes found in this
theme is the element selected for development with the principal motive.

Let us look at the development-section. For about fifty-five
measures, or half its length, it is concerned entirely with trans-
positions and sequences of the principal motive made into
single melodies or contrapuntal imitations between voices. At
the fifty-fifth measure the subsidiary theme described above
makes an authoritative appearance. This is repeated in another key. Beethoven then begins a series of sequences on the
first two long notes of this theme. All at once we discover
that one of the notes has disappeared. Now we have only one
note of our melody as part of a series of chords. The music
has become soft and mysterious. Suddenly the subsidiary
theme tries another vigorous entrance only to die away again,
this time in a very few measures. The principal motive bois-
terously interrupts and jubilantly continues to bring about a
return of the original key and its own first statement.

Even if we do not know exactly what is happening in this

development, we are aware of its dramatic quality. The effect is rather terrible, these soft detached chords and the fury of the returning motive. The importance of the principal motive is much enhanced by the simultaneous disintegration of the subsidiary one.

It must not be supposed that the devices of development which are listed here are an exhaustive statement of the possibilities of symphonic variation. No such list could ever be complete for, as it was being compiled, a new composer might very well be discovering new resources. It cannot even pretend to cover the field of music up to the end of the nineteenth century. Music is much too subtle an art to classify in any convenient arrangement. Nor do the characteristic tendencies of such men as Haydn, Beethoven and Brahms which are here suggested make it possible to pigeon-hole their music into convenient files. In the case of each of these composers, no single development is exactly like another in plan. We can only hope by analysing one or two to learn something of the composer's methods.

In conclusion, let us sum up the ten principal methods of development which we have discovered. Here is the list:

1. Transposition of melody or phrase or motive.
2. Variation of accompaniment of repeated melody.
3. Change of mode.
4. Melodic variation, by rhythmic change with retention of melodic outline, or by persistence of rhythm and change in succession of tones.
5. Theme combination with new material—with other themes already stated.
6. Augmentation and diminution of theme.

7. Polyphonic combination upon itself by canon and fugue.
8. Breaking up of theme into fragments to be separately developed.
9. Amplification of theme.
10. Disintegration of theme.

In examining the development-section of a symphonic movement, do not make the error of expecting all these ten types to appear. The majority of composers are content to employ only two or three in a single work. The simpler types are by far the most frequently encountered.

CHAPTER XII

Pre-Symphony Forms

IN our study so far we have been concerned with a close inspection of music phrase by phrase. We have seen how the elements combine to make an intelligible musical idea and that this idea often contains potentialities of musical development. If we have learned to recognize musical subject matter in original and varied state, we have made definite progress toward intelligent musical appreciation. We are now prepared to study the principal forms in which music is constructed. The advantage of further study is that it provides us with a musical framework; we shall know in a fashion what to expect from a composition in a given form. We shall still have to concentrate upon details of phrase, but with a knowledge of form we shall be able better to reconstruct these into a complete musical image.

Possibly at least seventy-five per cent of the music you hear will be in song-form, the simple ABA variety. Occasionally this will be expanded into five-part form as in the case of the Beethoven *Adagio Cantabile* from Opus 13. Songs themselves are either written in this form or in strophic form, the music repeated for each stanza of the verse. Rarely do we encounter a song of a more symphonic type such as Schubert's *Erl-King*.

Instrumental and choral music, on the other hand, use forms of greater variety and scope.

Most of the music heard in the ordinary concert comes from the nineteenth century. Bach, Handel, Haydn and Mozart are the most frequently encountered eighteenth-century composers, and only a few of the composers of our own century have earned their right to frequent performance. It is the nineteenth century, the great period of Romanticism, which still provides the majority of our programs. Since the most popular form of this age was the song-form, we already have considerable equipment to assist us. Suppose, however, we proceed historically, studying the instrumental forms as they developed.

Before 1600 there were no large forms peculiar to instrumental music. From this time on until the appearance of Haydn in the middle of the eighteenth century, there was continual experimentation on the part of composers in an attempt to discover designs capable of expansion which would serve as proper vehicles for characteristic instrumental effects. The first instrumental music imitated the polyphonic forms of choral music. The instrumental fugue was the product of this line of experimentation. We have seen that this form served as the chief medium for the larger instrumental works of Bach.

The first large form, which was invented for instrumental purposes alone, was the *Italian overture* found in the works of Monteverdi and Alessandro Scarlatti. The purpose of the overture was to prepare a somewhat restless audience for the rise of the curtain and the proper business of the evening. Early opera audiences did not take the opera overture any more seriously than our audiences do today. Conversation and general bustle which would be unforgivable after the rise of the curtain seem perfectly appropriate to the average audience.

The Italian overture which was often called *Sinfonia* or *Toccata* consisted of three parts, an *allegro*, a middle section in slow time and a second *allegro* which might or might not resemble the first part. This form was modified by Lulli in a series of opera and ballet works written about 1672 in which he began with a slow part, *lento* or *grave*, and followed it with an *allegro* in fugal style. Sometimes the original *grave* returned to conclude. This form, called the *French overture*, served as the basis of the opera overture up to the time of Wagner; it also had a great influence upon the first movement form of the symphony. You will find the opera overtures of Handel, Rameau, Purcell, and some of those of Gluck written in this style. Also the first movements of the four Bach orchestral suites which he called *Overtures* were written in this form.

Another form found in Bach and many composers of the classic period was the *Fantasia*. This was more or less unstandardized, but was sometimes built in fugal style. Today we often use the term *fantasia* for music which is so weak in unity of design as to unfit it for any other title, fantasias being usually nothing but potpourris of collected tunes, but the classic fantasia is a work of serious import. We sometimes find in these works a tendency toward the form which came later to be called sonata-form. This will be explained in the next chapter.

The *G minor Fantasia* of Bach which accompanies the

great *G minor organ fugue* is an example of this type. It consists of two definite themes: the first, an elaborate melodic figure with a strong rhythmic feeling, the second, a short and expressive melodic fragment which is polyphonically treated by imitation in the several voices. These two themes are alternately developed in the course of the work. Note particularly the tremendous climax which occurs in the central portion, with descending bass accompanied by a succession of chromatic harmonies. This composition shows Bach in his most magnificent vein. It is music of great power and originality.

If the old choral music produced the instrumental forms of the overture, the fugue and the fantasia, dance music exerted a still greater influence. Many of the familiar dance rhythms such as the gavotte and the minuet are of considerable antiquity. They probably took their shape originally from the folk song; a few related phrases and much repetition. As instrumental music progressed it was found that many repetitions of a short piece of music necessitated by the figuration of the dance was tiresome. In the case of the minuet, for instance, each couple would be expected to execute the dance in turn. Accordingly it was found that two similar dances played in alternation gave variety to the music. From this simple device come three important forms frequently encountered before Haydn and given a place in the symphony by him and succeeding composers.

The first of these forms varies a single dance or *refrain* with a number of others, the refrain alternating with each new section. This is the *rondo*. The refrain begins and ends the movement; the alternate sections are called *couplets*. This simple scheme is found in many composers of the time of Bach and

Handel, Couperin (1668–1733), Rameau (1683–1764), Domenico Scarlatti (1685–1757), as well as in the works of many of the Italian masters of the seventeenth century. It is a very simple form to follow, for the refrain in addition to returning regularly does not vary in its repetitions. Later on when the rondo appears in the sonata and symphony, we shall find some variation of refrain and some repetition between couplets.

An example of simple rondo is Couperin's *Soeur Monique* written for harpsichord. Here a tuneful refrain is alternated with couplets of a somewhat similar nature. Each statement of the refrain comes to a full cadence, and it is therefore easy to follow. There are four sections of the refrain and three sections of couplets. The last couplet is noticeably longer than the first two.

The second form is the *minuet* as distinct from other dances such as the gavotte and the pavan. It consists regularly of two dances known as the *minuet* and *trio*. These are arranged in the form ABA, the minuet serving as A, the trio as B. The explanation of the name given to the trio is that the middle dance was frequently played by a smaller number of instruments, generally three, for the sake of variety.

A popular example of the Minuet and Trio is the *Minuet in A major* from a string quintet of Boccherini (1743–1805). This is often transcribed for other instruments. The minuet and trio are each divided into two sections repeated separately. The trio, which is in the key of D major, consists of entirely different material from the minuet. At the conclusion of the trio, the minuet is played again without repeats.

The minuet was taken over into the symphony by Haydn

and his predecessors in Mannheim, and later developed at the hands of Beethoven into the *scherzo,* following the same general plan as before but accelerated in pace. In the minuets of Haydn and Mozart you will notice that the trio, which may or may not be in a different key from the minuet, is made up of entirely different material. Both the minuet and the trio are subdivided into two parts, each of which is repeated the first time through. When the minuet is played for the second time these repeats are generally omitted. In the music of Bach and Handel, the minuet often appears as a single dance without a trio.

The third form is the *theme and variations.* Originally it was called *air and double.* The double served to present the air in a varied arrangement, usually with added movement in the rhythm. A second double was sometimes found with still more elaboration of rhythm.

The classic *theme and variations* is usually based upon this procedure. A melody of four or eight phrases of a simple, tuneful nature is stated entire with final cadence. There follow parallel sections in which the accompaniment and the melody vary considerably. Enough of the original section will persist so that we can recognize the relationship of each variation to the original theme, but sometimes the melody and rhythm wander so far afield that the original scheme of the harmony is all that remains. This form is entertaining and easy to follow; its great disadvantage consists in the fact that each variation ends with a final cadence, and we often feel a lack of sustained interest between variations. A good example of this form is found in Handel's *Harmonious Blacksmith,* which is available, recorded for the instrument for which it was originally intended, the harpsichord. The theme consists of four phrases of which the third and fourth are repeated literally in the original statement. You will notice that each of the first three phrases has a suspensive cadence with the dominant chord.

The first variation brings us an alteration of the melody by the addition of extra notes. Whereas it was in eighth-notes, it is now in sixteenth-notes; yet we are entirely aware of the original melody contained in it. The second variation shifts the sixteenth-notes to the left hand and states the melody by the coöperation of two voices which form the upper part. First one voice has a note of the melody, then another. The third variation puts still more notes in the melody, using a triplet figure, but still it is readily distinguishable. The fourth variation follows the plan of the second with relation to the first, the triplet figure being in the left hand and the melody above. The fifth variation has so many notes in the right hand that the melody practically disappears. What remains intact is the original harmonic succession, and we have heard this so many times that this repeated element is sufficient to unite the variation with those that precede it. This fifth variation gives the harpsichordist a fine chance to display finger agility. One of the great hazards encountered by the theme and variations form is that it is an excellent vehicle for virtuoso music, and many variations are written to astonish with instrumental skill rather than to show the original theme in interesting new lights.

Somewhat like the theme and variations is another early instrumental form, the *passacaglia* or *chaconne*. It consists of variations on a fixed bass and differs from the theme and variations in that the bass does not change but in each successive variation new material in the upper voices is combined with the original bass. Occasionally the theme moves up into the upper voices for the sake of variety. In the case of the Bach *Passacaglia in C minor* for organ, one of his greatest works and one which we shall briefly examine, not only does the theme appear in the upper voices but in one of the variations it is slightly altered. The theme is so strong and fine that although there are twenty variations and a concluding fugue based upon it, we do not tire of the repetition, and the work is remarkably unified. The theme is stated alone to begin the composition. Several successful transcriptions of this work have been made for orchestra in which the polyphony is somewhat clearer than in the original organ version. In preferring one of these transcriptions to Bach's original we can at least offer the excuse that had the modern orchestra existed in Bach's time, he too might have preferred it as a medium for his large polyphonic works.

From earliest times of the composition of dance music a tendency to group separate dances together for purposes of contrast is to be observed. The *pavan* which was a slow stately dance would generally have a companion *galliard,* a somewhat more lively piece. No attempt was made to unify these two pieces save by key and contrast. They were separately played and consisted of different material. As instrumental music tended to exist for its own sake and not as mere accompaniment to song or dance, the grouping of a number of pieces in this relationship became a common practice. They were called *suites of lessons* in England, *partitas* in Germany, *ordres* in France and *sonatas* in Italy. Sonata was a term originally used to distinguish music for bowed instruments as opposed to *toccata,* music for keyboard instruments and *cantata,* music to be sung. We generally refer to these groups of pieces now as *suites*.

The suite gradually assumed a place of great importance in music which it held until the establishment of the sonata by Haydn. It consisted of any number of dances, generally at least six, all in the same key and designed to be played in succession, but detached. No attempt to unify the pieces was made, key and contrasting movement being their only relationship. The dance rhythms were selected from different countries and were so varied in their characteristics that an interesting succession of pieces resulted. As the suite became established, the dances gradually lost their relationship to their original dance movement and took on a purely instrumental aspect and a special form.

This form is interesting to us because it contains the germ of the idea of key contrast which is the principal element of sonata first-movement form as will be explained in the next chapter. The themes or subjects were seldom more than melodic and rhythmic patterns; concentrated motive, as we have seen it in the symphony and fugue, was practically unknown. The instrumental pattern proceeded for two or four phrases and came to a stop on a full cadence in another key. This key was the key of the dominant, if the piece was in major, or the key of the relative major if it was in minor. The first section was then repeated. The second section took up the figuration in the new key and by a process of simple development gradually modulated back to the original key where it ended, without, however, having stated the beginning of the theme or whatever was most noticeable about the figuration in the home key. The second section was then repeated.

This design is what we call *suite-form*. It is entirely archaic today. No music to speak of has been written in this fashion since the time of Haydn. But if we wish to understand the suites of Bach such as the *French Suites,* the *English Suites,* the *Partitas,* not to speak of his works known as sonatas; the instrumental works of Handel, Couperin and Rameau; the sonatas of Corelli (1653–1713), Vivaldi (d. 1743) and Domenico Scarlatti, we shall have to take it into account, for it and the fugue constituted the principal forms in general use before the time of Haydn.

It is easy to see why the typical suite-form became archaic. In the first place the absence of definite concentrated subjects makes the music sound much more vague than the symphony. But beyond this defect, there is the greater objection that in the plan of the suite our feeling for symmetry is unsatisfied. Even though the music which begins the piece may be vague in outline, we should like to hear it again at the end of the piece to complete the cycle of movement. To be sure, the arrangement of keys is designed to give us this effect. We pass from our tonic key to the dominant or relative, have a point of repose there, and in the second half of the piece we return to our home key. Tonality, however, is not a sufficient force by itself to give the composition that essential symmetry which we crave.

We shall find, if we study many examples of suite-form, that composers were often unsatisfied with this design themselves, and particularly in the case of the great Italian composer Corelli, a return of the theme is often found in the second part as well as more concentration of thematic subject matter. Although the sonatas of Corelli are not really sonatas at all but suites, we often feel very near to the sonata in listening to them. The return of the theme is sometimes found in Bach and in Scarlatti but it is the exception, not the rule.

As we have observed, all the pieces in the suite were in the same form and in the same key. This organization is very different from that of the sonata and symphony which consists of several different forms in contrasted keys. The suite, however, gradually established itself into successions of dances which have somewhat the same rhythmical character as the movements of the symphony. For instance, the suite usually begins with an *allemande,* a movement which did not have its origin at all in the dance but which was gradually evolved by the suite itself. It is a piece generally in 4/4 time of moderate rapidity. Generally speaking this movement of the suite, like the first movement of the symphony, is most serious in style.

The second movement of the suite, the *courante,* has no counterpart in the symphony. It is in 3/2 or 3/4 time and moves more rapidly than the allemande. Also it is generally more polyphonic in style. The slow movement of the symphony is suggested by the third movement of the suite, the *sarabande*. This is a slow, lyric piece in triple rhythm. The sarabande is almost always the most expressive movement of the suite.

The sarabande is generally followed by one or more pieces more purely dancelike in character. These dance movements have their exact parallel in the minuet and scherzo of the symphony. There is a great variety of them to be found in the usual suite. Some of the more common ones are the *gavotte,* the *minuet,* the *bourrée,* the *loure,* the *scherzo,* the *polonaise,* and the *burlesca.* These names must not be confused with works of later composers called by the same names. When found in the suite they are usually in the typical suite-form.

The last movement of the suite is generally a *gigue* or *giga,* a lively piece customarily in 6/8 time or some other variant of triple rhythm such as 3/8, 12/8, etc. As suggested by its title it has a close relationship to the rollicking rhythm known as the jig. Sometimes gigues as well as dances, such as the gavotte, are found separately in rondo rather than suite-form. When appearing in the suite, however, they are generally in the usual two-part form.

Suites were written as a rule for either the harpsichord, a solo instrument accompanied by harpsichord, or a group of stringed or wind instruments. A good example of the harpsichord suite is the *G major Suite* from the *French Suites* of Bach. The successive movements are *Allemande, Courante, Sarabande, Gavotte, Bourrée, Loure* and *Gigue.* This music is largely polyphonic in texture in spite of its simple dance pattern. You will find it, however, melodious and gay, and the *Sarabande* is one of the loveliest examples of the type. Notice that the rhythmic idea of the first two bars constantly develops by transposition and melodic variation.

Another type of composition in several movements which appears in the early eighteenth-century literature is the *concerto.* This may consist of three or more movements in related but not necessarily identical keys. The forms used in the early concerto show considerable variety, but they are all based upon the principle of imitation between solo or group of soloists and accompanying body. This relationship of give and take between two bodies of instrumentalists or singers is called *antiphony*. Frequently in the typical concerto movement, a refrain will be stated by the ensemble marked *tutti* and will be succeeded by developed fragments marked *solo* which modulate. Statements of the refrain occurring in different keys will be alternated with further solo passages.

The eighteenth-century concerto must not be confused with the virtuoso concerto resembling the symphony which first appears in the works of Mozart and finds so many examples in the literature of the nineteenth century. In the eighteenth-century concerto we find two types, the *Solo Concerto* and the *Concerto Grosso*. In the case of the former one instrument, or at the most two (*vide* Bach *Concerto for two violins*) are accompanied by a group of strings and harpsichord. In the Concerto Grosso, the solo group may comprise several instruments, winds or strings, or combinations of both used in antiphonal relationship with the accompanying body of strings and harpsichord.

As an example of the Concerto Grosso, the one in F major of Handel is available in records and may be regarded as typical. Also the six *Brandenburg Concertos* of Bach, which are unsurpassed examples of the form, are all recorded. The *E major Concerto for Violin and Strings*, also available on records, is a beautiful example of the solo concerto.

We sometimes find a concerto written for a single instrument, the harpsichord or the organ. Bearing in mind the fact that the harpsichord like the organ had more than one keyboard and several tone colors, we can easily understand how these instruments could reproduce the antiphonal effect typical of the concerto. This explains such a work as the *Italian Concerto* of Bach which was written for solo harpsichord, but which is played today with some loss of original intention on a solo piano.

One other category of pieces remains to be explained for those who are interested in the instrumental works of Bach. The organ fugues and the fugues in the *Well-Tempered Clavichord* are always preceded by a companion piece, generally a *prelude*. We have already explained the fantasia which sometimes appears. The *toccata* which is also found is generally a piece of rapid figuration which proceeds in a plan of tonality like the fugue without much concentration of thematic material or contrast.

The form of the prelude may be any one of the types we have found. The name has no especial formal significance. In the *Well-Tempered Clavichord* we find suite-form, song-form and something resembling the fantasia or toccata, a sequence of tonalities, such as is the rule for the fugue, embodying a rhythmic figuration. This last type is found in the famous *C major prelude* in the first book which Gounod undertook to provide with a melody.

The overture, the suite, the fugue, and the concerto, the principal early instrumental forms are important not only because of the great literature which exemplifies them, but also because they each made significant contribution to the principal instrumental forms of the later eighteenth and nineteenth centuries, the Sonata and the Symphony.

CHAPTER XIII

The Classic Symphony

IT is customary to call the last half of the eighteenth century the classic period of music. The use of the term classic for all music which is not popular ballad or dance music is confusing and is to be avoided. Schumann and Wagner may be great composers established in critical esteem for many years, but they are composers of the romantic age, not the classic. Educated people usually assume that the term music means serious music, and if it is necessary to distinguish between this and popular ballads or dance tunes, the latter may be called popular music. To group all music which does not come under the head of popular music as classical is a mark of lack of cultivation.

The reason why we think of the age of Haydn and Mozart as the classic period is that during these years instrumental forms were definitely fixed. Not only do we find here the framework upon which all subsequent music has been built, but we also discover that here for the first time instrumental groupings, such as the symphony orchestra, the string quartet and the chamber ensemble, were standardized.

It seems hard to realize that the symphony orchestra as we know it did not come at once. On the contrary, the orchestras which accompanied the early operas varied enormously. The basis of the orchestra was the harpsichord; the players were kept together when necessary by signals from the harpsichordist much in the fashion that the obsolescent theatre orchestra is directed by a pianist who occasionally raises a free hand to give a down beat to his colleagues. To one or several harpsichords the composer would add those instruments which he thought necessary for the dramatic effects of the work. It was not until Lulli (1633–1687) assembled a group of winds and strings that a body somewhat like our symphony orchestra came into being.

Even after Lulli, orchestras depended somewhat upon the purse of the noble who kept the players as a part of his retinue. Bach in his work at Coethen where he was court composer, or at Leipzig where he provided church music, never had what we should recognize as a full orchestra. You will notice this if you watch the grouping of players used to accompany the *Mass in B minor* or to play one of the Brandenburg concertos.

Haydn (1732–1809), however, was so fortunate as to be employed by the wealthy Prince Esterhazy, who gave him enough players so that he was able to standardize certain groups and write works for them which served as the basis for all succeeding compositions. To the typical orchestra of Haydn, consisting of flutes, oboes, bassoons, trumpets, horns, strings and kettle drums, Mozart added the clarinets and the trombones; thus we have the model for the great Wagnerian orchestra of the nineteenth century.

Some time before the appearance of Haydn, the viol family had been definitely displaced by the louder and more effective violin type. In Haydn's time the harpsichord gave way to the louder and more rhythmic piano. Practically all the instruments which we have today existed in fairly complete form in the classic age. The brass instruments were made without valves and consequently were unable to play all the notes of the scale, but this limitation was somewhat compensated for by the skill and adroitness of the classic composers in using them. The classic symphony orchestra, which today is often reproduced in the concert hall for performances of the Haydn and Mozart symphonies, differs chiefly in volume from the one required for modern works.

During the first half of the eighteenth century and before, music for ensemble of instruments was invariably accompanied by a keyboard instrument, generally the harpsichord. This instrument furnished a harmonic background which served to bind together the fabric of the music. Curiously the part furnished the player was not written out, but consisted merely of the bass, above the notes of which were written figures indicating the harmony to be played. This device was known as *figured bass*. You will find it in the concertos of Bach, Handel, Corelli, in the so-called sonatas of the period, in the early symphonies and even in the accompaniments to choral music. There was no distinction made between chamber music and music for large orchestra. Doubling of parts, whatever the nomenclature of the composition, was the usual practice, and as we have seen, the number of players available usually determined the size of the ensemble.

The dividing line between the old and the new conception of ensemble came when the figured bass part was written out or entirely omitted. We notice then two main tendencies. The doubling of parts and standardization of instrumentation became the orchestral principle. The reduction of players to one for a part and careful attention to independent part writing became the chamber music principle. We have then, in Haydn's time, the first genuine distinction made between chamber and orchestral music. In the category of chamber music we find the trio, quartet, quintet, and sonata for one or more instruments. In the realm of the orchestra we find the symphony, the overture, and the concerto.

The general design and the forms employed in this new music greatly resembled one another. They represent a fusion and extension of preceding forms, the French and Italian overture, the concerto, the suite and the fugue. These forms were developed and standardized by the composers of the so-called Mannheim School, Stamitz, Richter, and others, and the Viennese composers Haydn and Mozart. Although modifications are to be observed in succeeding composers, the principles of the classic composers, once established, have continued as the basis of all instrumental music in the larger forms.

As a rule compositions were grouped into three or four movements. These movements, as in the suite and the concerto, had no thematic relationship but were combined purely upon the principles of key relationship and rhythmic contrast. Various forms were used in the different movements, but the most typical and the one capable of the greatest expansion was a new form, called *sonata-form,* or sometimes because it is generally found in the first movement of the sonata and the symphony, *first-movement-form.*

This form has a resemblance to the simple ABA design of the folk song in that the first and third sections greatly resemble each other. The middle section, however, as we have studied, consists of a working out or development of the material of the exposition instead of new and contrasting material. The first or *exposition-section* states the principal themes, and the third or *recapitulation-section* restates them. There is an important distinction between them, however. The first section, like the suite, is concerned with two tonalities and a modulation. The first theme (A) is presented in the tonic key, a modulation occurs to the key of the dominant or relative major, and a second theme (B) is heard in the newly established tonality. The middle section generally employs a number of tonalities, but in the course of its unfolding gradually reëstablishes the tonic key. The recapitulation-section contains no modulation but presents all the material in the central tonality of the movement. Preceding the movement there is often a slow introduction as in the French overture which may or may not have thematic relationship to the principal material of the movement. After the recapitulation there is sometimes appended a coda. The usual tempo of the main body of the movement is allegro.

We have observed that the form of the suite did not satisfy the instinct for symmetry which likes to have the original theme appear in the home key at the end of the movement, and that certain composers provided for this by so stating it. Suite-form then changed from a two-part form (statement of theme and modulation serving as first part, and working out with modulation back to the home key as second), to a three-part design where the theme restated without modulation provided the third section. This design is somewhat like three-part song-form, the fundamental design of almost all music. The difference is chiefly that instead of the middle part being contrasting material, it is development of the original theme; in other words it is more symphonic. Also there is not exact repetition between the first and third sections because there is a modulation in the first part which, if the piece is to end in the right key, must not be repeated in the third.

Philip Emmanuel Bach (1714–1788), the second son of the great Bach and choirmaster at the court of Frederick the Great, is generally credited with the innovation necessary to change this form into completed sonata-form. In several of his harpsichord sonatas, he adds to the first part a second theme which serves as the device to modulate away from the home key, so that A, or the first theme, may be the same in both sections in which it appears. This makes the form A–B (with modulation), development, and A–B (without modulation). For purposes of contrast, B was designed to be lyric as opposed to A which was customarily rhythmic in character.

The importance of this somewhat arbitrary design is that it is capable of indefinite expansion. If you examine the three parts, you will notice that the only place where a full cadence in the home key could arrive is at the ending of the third section. Song-form on the other hand seems to indicate such a cadence at the end of the first section, and there is always the danger that this ending will not carry the interest over to the second and third sections. The sections of a musical design are somewhat like the acts of a play. If the play does not provide situations which carry the interest forward from act to act, the design is faulty and the play generally unsuccessful. The design of sonata-form has proved to be ideal for extended musical works; in the history of music no other pattern has been discovered to displace it.

It took much experimentation upon the part of Haydn, Mozart and their contemporaries before this form was standardized. In the early symphonies of Haydn, the form is less clear and the relationship of first and second theme is not fully established. For example, you will find that in the first section of sonata-form, after modulating away from the key of A, he restates A in the new key before stating the second theme. This minimizes the importance of B which is sometimes hardly recognizable as a theme, but mere figuration. Another great difficulty in the manipulation of sonata-form is the treatment of the modulation which is necessary in the first section between A and B, but not required in the recapitulation-section where both themes are to appear in the same key. The recapitulation-sections of the early classic symphonies often contain passages which are not at all clear as the composer attempts to solve this difficulty.

As the form approached perfection it was found that the first section modulation could be achieved best not by one of the two principal themes, but by additional figuration which need not be repeated in the third section; this material was called the *bridge* or *transition section*. In Haydn and Mozart it is seldom of much thematic importance and often resembles one or another of the themes, but Beethoven generally uses the bridge for the statement of additional material to be used in the development-section. Brahms, who is especially expert at the manufacture of smooth joints, often makes it of a blend of material from the two themes so that the transition from one theme to another is scarcely perceptible.

When there is a bridge of thematic importance so that it must be restated in the third section of sonata-form, the composer may do one of two things. He can alter it so that it appears to modulate, but really brings back the same key, or he can alter the end of the first theme so that the bridge is necessary to bring back the proper key. Often the bridge is entirely omitted in the recapitulation-section, but if this is the case one of the two principal themes must be lengthened so that the general proportions of the section will resemble those of the first.

Another expansion of the form is easily explained. If the second theme is to be lyric and expressive, it does not serve as a very good ending of the section, for this must be decisive so that the arrival of the development-section will be noticed. Accordingly a theme designed to bring about a suitable closing is generally added to B. This is in the same key as B, and in the recapitulation it must also be transposed into the home key. To avoid confusion let us call the proper second theme B1 and the closing theme B2 so that we can regard as the B section all the material stated in the second key.

Mozart (1756–1791) was a much younger man than Haydn, but died many years before him. When Mozart began composing, Haydn had sufficiently progressed so that his works served as a model for the younger man. Each had great admiration for the other and admitted reciprocal influence. Mozart was blessed with an instinct for form as great as his facility for composition. His treatment of the sonata-form was more concise than Haydn's. The older man recognized this and during the latter period of Haydn's life we find his best work bearing the stamp of certain Mozart innovations. One of these was a greater clarity and expressiveness given to the second theme. The first theme disappeared from the B or transposed section and B1 and B2 came to have greater importance. Another innovation was the increased importance given to the end of the movement. Although we find many Mozart first movements coming to a rapid close after the recapitulation of B1 and 2 in the home key, often he adds a *coda* which is a sort of second development of great importance to the composition. In Beethoven it comes to have still greater importance in the general scheme. Mozart, also, often omits the slow introduction at the start of the movement.

Let us make a chart of the sonata-form as found in the most important symphonies of Haydn and Mozart:

EXPOSITION-SECTION

Slow introduction (*optional*)	Theme A in home key	Bridge passage (*modulates*)	Theme B1 B2 Closing theme (*key of dominant or relative*)

DEVELOPMENT-SECTION

Working out of motives selected from the above in various keys.

RECAPITULATION-SECTION

Theme A in home key	Bridge passage (*altered or omitted*)	Theme B1	Closing theme B2 (*in the home key*)	Coda (*optional*)

With this chart in mind it might be of value to play over the whole of the first movement of the Mozart G minor Symphony, the development of which we have already

studied. There is no slow introduction, but there is a short
coda where the material of A is given additional development. The bridge theme is very important and the actual
modulation is done by A before it is reached. If you listen
closely you will hear traces of the bridge rhythm used to accompany some development of A in the working-out section.
The second theme is lyric, a melodic figure based upon
three descending notes of the chromatic scale; it is stated after
a rest interval of one bar. This theme is of considerable extent
and contains more material than the short motive which begins it. The closing theme bears some rhythmic resemblance
to A. In the recapitulation-section the bridge is lengthened
and developed. Since B1 and B2 first appear in the relative
major, their change to the home key of G minor makes them
quite different in effect.

So far we have discussed only the first movement of the
sonata and the symphony. What of the others? We have
seen that the instrumental suite is organized with rhythmic
contrast, unity of tonality and similarity of form. The sonata
and symphony (for our purposes they may be considered as
identical in organization) substitute for unity of tonality a
series of related tonalities with the first and last movements
in the central tonality, and for similarity of form considerable variety in the various movements. Sonata-form may
appear in other movements beside the first, but when appearing in the second or the last movement, especially in the
classic symphony, thematic material is usually less concentrated and the movement tends to be somewhat shorter.

The second movement, like the sarabande, is generally

characterized by melodic expressiveness and is generally in the tempo of an *andante* or an *adagio*. In the symphonies and sonatas of Haydn and Mozart, any one of three forms may appear; sonata-form, song-form, or theme and variations.

The third movement is invariably minuet-form as outlined in the last chapter. We notice two types of minuets and trios, those resembling the suite in which the initial A does not return with the reëstablishment of the tonic key in the second section, and those which are more like song-form and include a return of A in the tonic. This type is more frequently encountered. Whether or not the initial melodic figure returns, the division of both minuet and trio is always made after the modulation so that minuet and trio consist each of two sections. As previously explained, the sections of minuet and trio are repeated the first time through, but in the return of the minuet these repeats are suppressed.

TYPE ONE

MINUET	TRIO
(*First Part*)	(*Second Part*) (*new material*)
SECTION A Theme, modulation, cadence.	SECTION A Theme, modulation, cadence.
(*Repeated*)	(*Repeated*)
SECTION B Development, modulation back to tonic without return of principal theme, cadence.	SECTION B Development, modulation back to tonic without return of principal theme, cadence.
(*Repeated*)	(*Repeated*)

The third part is identical with the first with the omission of the repeats.

TYPE TWO

MINUET	TRIO
(*First Part*)	(*Second Part*) (*new material*)
SECTION A Theme, modulation, cadence.	SECTION A Theme, modulation, cadence.
(*Repeated*)	(*Repeated*)
SECTION B Development, modulation back to tonic including return of principal theme.	SECTION B Development, modulation back to tonic, including return of principal theme.
(*Repeated*)	(*Repeated*)

The third part is identical with the first with the omission of the repeats.

The fourth movement may be sonata-form, a simple rondo (rare) or a combination form called *rondo-sonata*. (Theme and variations is infrequently found.) The rondo-sonata differs from the simple rondo in that there is unification of the couplets; the first couplet, stated in the key of the dominant or relative, may consist of several themes. Later in the piece it reappears in the key of the tonic. Refrains also tend somewhat to vary in this form, in contrast to the rondo where they are never changed in the course of the movement. It differs from sonata-form in that there is seldom a development-section, but instead new material is brought forward to form the central couplet.

Rondo-sonata

A; B (in new key); A; C; A; B (in tonic key); A.

Sometimes A is sufficiently varied to be called A′. The form may be extended by the addition of another couplet made of the B material. and A, serving as coda.

In listening to the classic symphony we must bear in mind that it is entirely different in scope from the symphony of Beethoven and Brahms, and was conceived for a very different audience. The late eighteenth century was an age of formalism where deep feeling was somewhat distrusted. Had one of Prince Esterhazy's audiences been given a performance of such a work as the *Pathetic Symphony* of Tschaikowsky, it would have been much surprised by its length, noisiness and excess of emotion. Tschaikowsky's music was prepared for by the great expansion of musical form and content which Beethoven and his successors provided. If we are at first inclined to regard the classic symphony as cold and formal, we should try to imagine ourselves back in an age which preferred more restrained expression. The gracefulness, good taste and elegant proportions of classic music are qualities which wear well. Perhaps you will find them an antidote to many things of a later origin which seem to you somewhat vulgar.

The classic symphony was much shorter than the symphony of the nineteenth century. This explains the difference in volume of output between Haydn and Mozart on the one hand, and Beethoven and Brahms on the other. Haydn wrote about one hundred and forty-three symphonies during his long life, Mozart in a much shorter span wrote forty-one. Mozart wrote so fast we are told that he composed his most popular three symphonies, the G minor, the E flat major and the C major in the space of six weeks one summer. Beethoven wrote only nine symphonies and Brahms four. Brahms worked for ten years on his first symphony before he gave it to the public. Undoubtedly the classic symphonies were often perfunctorily made. They were intended for a single occasion and many of them were not repeated. The idea of printing and wide circulation was very far from the composers' minds.

Among Haydn's and Mozart's works, and indeed in the case of later composers, we find short collections of pieces under a single heading which are really little symphonies and resemble the larger type in general construction. Such works are called *Serenades* or *Divertimentos*. A very famous example of this is Mozart's serenade, *Eine Kleine Nachtmusik*.

The *overture* as found in Mozart's operas varies. We find such an example as that of *The Magic Flute* which is very much like the old French overture: slow introduction and fugal allegro. The Overture to *The Abduction from the Seraglio* is an excellent example of the old Italian overture. The very frequently heard Overture to *The Marriage of Figaro,* however, is like the first movement of a symphony, with practically all development-section omitted. Gradually the overture became a recognized form as found in examples of Weber, Beethoven and occasionally in Wagner. It retained the slow introduction of the old overture, but took sonata-form as its model for the allegro. In addition there is often a dramatic episode from the opera contained in it, something not to be explained in terms of sonata-form. This episode is found in the development as in the Overture to *Euryanthe* or at the end as in the Overture to *Egmont*.

It is important to distinguish between the terms *sonata* and *sonata-form*. The sonata, as we have already explained, is a group of pieces under a single heading like the symphony. These pieces are somewhat loosely related, but are customarily played in succession. They are not all in the same key, as in the case of the suite, but are in related tonalities, the first and the last movements generally being in the same key and the other movements in neighboring tonalities. The first movement of a sonata is generally in a special form which was the characteristic contribution of the sonata to musical design, hence called sonata-form. The other movements, as explained above, vary in design. In the classic symphony and sonata, no attempt was made to unify the various parts of the composition one to another. A single movement could be played from a symphony and stand as a composition by itself. Movements from several symphonies if in proper tonal relationship could be, and in fact sometimes were, played as a single symphony.

CHAPTER XIV

The Symphony of the Nineteenth Century

IT would not be possible to include within the scope of this study even a bare outline of the history of the symphony of the nineteenth century. What particularly concerns us is the symphonic framework, not its history. Perhaps it is easier to study this framework as it was built up from composer to composer, confining ourselves to those men who were responsible for its growth.

There is not a single tendency of the nineteenth century which we do not find at least suggested in the works of Beethoven (1770–1827). He is to the symphony what Bach is to the fugue. If we can understand the large symphonic canvas of Beethoven, no other symphonies written before or since should lie beyond our grasp.

We have already remarked upon the conception, different from the classic symphony, which is indicated by such features as subject matter and plan of development in the Beethoven symphony. It remains to enumerate some further details of design which appear as innovations in his work.

Beethoven studied composition for a time with Haydn, and as might be expected, his early compositions show the clear imprint of his teacher's hand. The first two symphonies follow not only the design, but the style of the Haydn symphony; all the movements are in sonata-form with the exception of the third movement of each. The third movement of the First Symphony suggests a typical Haydn minuet, but the third movement of the Second Symphony is a *scherzo* somewhat more characteristic of Beethoven's own personality. Although the form of the scherzo is like that of the minuet, its character undergoes a profound metamorphosis. The gay minuet of Haydn and Mozart is nothing like the impetuous, headlong Beethovenian scherzo. The word *scherzo* means jest; Beethoven's jesting is what you would expect from the man himself, rough and uncouth, but tremendously vital. His jesting reaches a climax in the scherzo of the Ninth Symphony which is playful somewhat as a Jove is playful, hurling thunderbolts at mortals below.

From the Third Symphony on, Beethoven writes out the third section of the scherzo instead of indicating by the sign *da capo* that the first part is to be repeated literally. The Fifth Symphony scherzo has a third section in which the presentation of the first section material is greatly changed; also this scherzo does not come to an end, but is joined to the last movement. In a number of the later scherzos, the form becomes five parts with two appearances of the trio and three of the scherzo proper. He also adds a short coda to the end of the piece, generally containing a reminiscence of the trio. The Eighth Symphony, which is a reversion to the classic pattern, is an exception to the above, and the third movement has again the characteristic features of the Haydn minuet, with the use of the *da capo* sign for literal repetition of the first part.

The changed aspect of the third movement had a somewhat disturbing effect upon the proportions of the symphony as conceived by Haydn. The lilting, tuneful rondo followed very naturally after the dignified dance rhythm of the minuet, but the scherzo steals some of the fire of the classic rondo and leaves the last movement with the necessity of establishing another mood. As a result the last movement grew in importance until, in some cases, it was sufficiently serious to compete with the first movement. In the Ninth Symphony Beethoven put the scherzo movement second so that the joyful finale comes as a marked contrast to the lyric and leisurely third movement.

But it is in sonata-form itself that the greatest change is to be noticed. We find great expansion of length, the inclusion of additional material and yet a greater degree of compactness of design. This compactness is a result of Beethoven's conception of form as something dramatic, and his use of thematic contrasts which furnish material for lengthy development. Even in the longest sonata-form movements of Beethoven, nothing is included which does not serve the main idea. The general procedure is to alternate the moods of themes; a rhythmically vigorous idea is usually succeeded by an expressive one of melodic character. The most salient of these themes are selected for treatment in the development-section. There is no padding; no episodes are included merely because they sound well. The main purpose of the movement is always in view.

The first section of the form, that devoted to statement of the themes, is different from that of Haydn and Mozart because of greater clarity of themes. You will never be in doubt as to what constitutes the principal theme of one of Beethoven's movements in sonata-form. When the theme has been stated he proceeds at once to the bridge where we often find an idea of much thematic importance. With the arrival of the new key a second theme is stated, generally lyric in character. This theme is sometimes regarded merely as a lyric interlude to form a contrast with the principal theme, but seldom to appear in the development-section. More often the principal material for development is contained in the first theme and the bridge. After the second theme (B1) there are generally two closing themes (B2 and B3). These may contain material related to the first theme or the bridge. Sometimes one of them is used to introduce the development-section.

In the matter of tonality of the exposition-section of sonata-form, Beethoven takes more liberties than were tolerated in the classic symphony where dominant or relative was the invariable rule. He never introduces remote keys in this section, however, and in the recapitulation he follows the classic practice of presenting all the material in a single key.

The Third Symphony, one of the longest, has an innovation which only appears once in all the symphonies, an innovation which has caused endless trouble to explain. He introduces a new theme in the middle of the development-section. It bears no resemblance to anything contained in the exposition-section. Perhaps it does as well as anything to say that at that point Beethoven needed another theme to contrast with his powerful first theme; there was no place to include it in the exposition so he simply stated it when he was ready to use it for development. It is a singularly lovely theme, one that you will easily recognize if you play through the movement.

The Beethovenian coda assumes great proportions; sometimes it is even more interesting than the development-section. He regards it as a second development; further conclusions to be drawn about his material after it has been restated in the recapitulation.

Here is the general plan of Beethoven's treatment of sonata-form as found in a number of his larger works:

1. Exposition of principal themes stated in terms of contrast.
2. Development of the most important themes.
3. Recapitulation showing variation of themes as affected by development.
4. Further development completely establishing one theme as victor.

All forms and all movements suffer changes at the hands of Beethoven. In the second movement there is a tendency away from sonata-form to song-form. It is, however, a somewhat symphonic song, often in five sections and containing development of themes. In three of the symphonies, the Fifth, Seventh and Ninth, the slow movement is a theme or double theme and variations; these are nothing like the loosely connected pieces of the classic age, the divisions are carefully concealed and the relation of variation to theme is often very subtle. The third movement, as described above, was changed from the Second Symphony on from minuet to scherzo, retaining in general the form of the minuet. In the last movement we find sonata-form, rondo-sonata, or theme and variations. For the finale of the Ninth Symphony which is a theme and variations of great length, a chorus is employed for the time in the history of the symphony; the text is Schiller's *Ode to Joy*.

The use of voices as an additional resource of the symphony was regarded by Beethoven's contemporaries as very daring. Indeed, of the later composers of the nineteenth century only Mahler has employed this innovation, but we shall see that this step of Beethoven's was of profound influence in the case of Wagner.

So much for the separate movements of the Beethoven symphonies. They are not hard to follow provided you hear the exposition-section frequently enough to become familiar with the themes. It is interesting as you listen to one of these expositions to speculate upon the choice of themes for development and what their rôle will be. In this way you will gain much insight into the mind of the composer.

In the problem of relationship of the movements constituting the symphony, Beethoven evidently felt an impulse toward unification. Early in the century potpourri symphonies with movements collected from different works were often played. The inter-relationship of movements of the symphony, linking them not only by means of tonality but by certain resemblances of themes, served to make the succession of movements more logical. This is what we call the *cyclic* treatment of themes in the symphony. There are a few traces of this in some of the early works of Beethoven; for example in the *Pathetic Sonata* Opus 13, the second theme of the first movement is the basis for the rondo refrain of the finale. In the scherzo of the Fifth Symphony there appears a theme which is rhythmically similar to the principal motive of the first movement. The relation between this scherzo and the finale is very close; the scherzo does not end but leads into the finale, and in the course of this movement it reappears as a part of the development-section.

It is in the Ninth Symphony, however, that we have the most surprising cyclic treatment of themes. In the long introduction to the last movement, one by one the themes of the preceding movements appear, led by a sort of conductor theme, until finally the theme proper ushers in the main body of the movement. This statement of the most important previous themes seems to sum up the whole symphony and tie it together.

Whether or not Beethoven intended to prescribe this unification as necessary to the symphony is not known. Certain composers who succeeded him, notably César Franck and his school, seized upon the idea as one of great importance and used themes interchangeably between movements. When carried too far, this leads to monotony. If a theme is much developed in the first movement, we are glad to pass on to fresh material when we come to the second. But if used with reticence, as Beethoven himself employed it, theme reminiscence from movement to movement adds to the unity of the whole work.

We have observed that in the classic period, the sonata, the string quartet and the symphony resemble each other in form. In the early work of Beethoven this resemblance is usually to be noted. In later compositions, particularly in the last period of his creative activity, when his deafness led to much introspection and a highly idealized form of music, certain differences are found. In the string quartets sometimes we find more than the customary four movements, often linked together without pause. Also the fugue interests him more and more as a separate form. There are several fugues used as sections of the quartets, there is also a separate composition for string quartet called *Great Fugue* which was originally intended as the finale to one of them, but discarded as too long.

In the sonatas we have the first appearance of the undiluted personality of the composer. Even at the period of his two first symphonies, when he was still strongly influenced by Haydn, he was bringing about changes in the piano sonata. Some of the features distinguishing the sonata from the symphony in Beethoven's work are irregularity of the number of movements (the last sonata, Opus 111, contains but two movements); variation in type of movement to begin the sonata (Opus 27 the *Moonlight Sonata* begins with a movement in modified song-form and Opus 26 begins with a theme and variation); linking together of separate movements; the inclusion of short connecting movements between two long ones; and several movements in fugue form. The last sonatas furnish several examples of theme and variations, where relationship of sections is so perfectly achieved that a new form may be said to have been created.

If we are to choose a single standard of form, Beethoven is not so satisfactory a master as Haydn. Although his musical architecture is far greater, his form tended to be increasingly subjective; it became the expression of his own thoughts, something personal and suited to his individual style of subject matter. Although he dominated every composer who came after him and seemed to exemplify every discovery of the century, he is entirely unstandardized. When we think that we have grasped the essential nature of his method, we are sure to come upon a work which refuses to be included in such a system. Accordingly Haydn, simple and objective as he is, remains the best model for symphonic writing. Many composers who have found in Beethoven their chief inspiration, also give evidence that they did not neglect the basic principles of Haydn and the classic sonata-form.

Of these composers of the symphony, Brahms (1833–1897) is easily the most important. Many of the romantic composers such as Schubert (1797–1828), Schumann (1810–1856), and Mendelssohn (1809–1847) composed symphonies which if less important than those of Beethoven, especially from an architectural point of view, have won an enduring place in the concert repertory.

Schubert wrote eight symphonies. The first six are classic in style and bear closer relationship to the symphonies of Haydn than to those of Beethoven. They are, however, of great lyric beauty and it is surprising that they appear so seldom on concert programs. The eighth symphony in B minor, known as the *Unfinished Symphony,* is an extraordinary composition in two movements. These combine Schubert's genius for melody and for the dramatic. For some reason he never added the third and fourth movements although sketches exist which indicate that he had planned to do so.

The seventh symphony in C major, composed after the eighth, is the longest and most important of his works in this form. The texture of the writing is less compact than that of Beethoven and the material lacks his power of concentration, but the themes are so beautiful that questions of form and style become rather futile when applied to a consideration of the work. From beginning to end this symphony is marked by sustained and joyous lyricism.

The four symphonies of Schumann contain much beautiful music which is somewhat handicapped by his comparative lack of skill in orchestration. Schumann's genius for form which is everywhere evident in his shorter works seems less adapted to the extended lengths of the symphony. Particularly in his treatment of first movement form we feel that like Schubert he is somewhat at a disadvantage, often confused or even pedantic. Generally the slow movements and scherzo are where he excels, but even there he is not always effective orchestrally. Schumann's greatest work for orchestra is his piano concerto, where his natural gift for writing for the instrument gives momentum and authority to the whole. Many musicians consider this the finest piano concerto in the literature of music.

The two most frequently played symphonies of Mendelssohn are the *Scotch* and *Italian* Symphonies. Mendelssohn was considered a classicist by his contemporaries. It was he who discovered some of the forgotten choral works of Bach and gave them to the public. He was a skilled and erudite composer, an artist of subtle delicacy and aristocratic charm. His symphonies are written with an almost perfect understanding of the resources of the orchestra. If, in general, the texture is not so compact nor the development so interesting as the symphonic style of Beethoven, the first movement of the *Italian Symphony* must be cited as an exception. This entire movement is related to, and penetrated by, the joyous, youthful motive which begins it.

With the appearance of Brahms some years later, the symphony came into a great renaissance. Not since the time of Bach had there been a composer who had so thoroughly assimilated all forms and styles of his predecessors. In the midst of the Romantic movement, in the very shadow of Wagner's overwhelming popularity, Brahms coolly surveyed the music of all the ages, including that of his own, and selected those elements which seemed to him most congenial. At a time when program music was the rage, he furnished no explanatory material about his work and confined himself to objective forms.

From Bach and the sixteenth-century masters he selected polyphonic treatment as opposed to the homophony in vogue. From the Middle Ages he gained his interest in the ancient modes, often flavoring his melodies with these melodic intervals. From the classic masters he took his solidity of design, and from Beethoven his manipulation of themes and logic of development. His was not a dramatic talent so we do not feel in the developments of Brahms that breathless excitement and cataclysmic tragedy which sometimes characterizes the music of Beethoven, but his music is probably the most compact of all, its logic derived from beautifully calculated development of contrasting musical designs. Every note of Brahms can be explained in terms of music alone. His music always sounds rich in texture, never bare and ugly as is sometimes the case in Beethoven.

If Beethoven is more elemental and tempestuous, Brahms creates a music which is invariably exalted and inspired.

Both composers excel in humanity and tenderness. Brahms sounds warmer perhaps than his predecessor because he uses the rich harmonies of the age of romantic music.

The innovations which Brahms brings to the form of the symphony are not many. Chief among them is his treatment of the dance movement which in each of his four symphonies is placed third in the group of four. He uses neither the Beethovenian scherzo, which was not at all sympathetic to his nature, nor the archaic minuet of Haydn. His dance is a slower, sweeter dance with the melodious quality of the folk song. For the form he uses a variant of simple song-form.

In the first movement Brahms discards the additional closing theme employed by Beethoven, confining himself, as did Haydn, to one. As with Beethoven, the bridge is of great importance. The First Symphony begins with a magnificent slow introduction in which the principal motives of the movement appear, but the other three symphonies begin at once with the *allegro*. In the Third Symphony the first two bars contain a motive which is used as a sort of motto for the movement; it appears in augmentation in the development and is stated between the second and closing themes in both the exposition and recapitulation. The coda, as with Beethoven, is important in all the symphonies.

The First Symphony of Brahms is much more polyphonic than the others, particularly in the first movement. It is based upon the two motives stated in the introduction; these two motives form *double counterpoint,* that is, each may be stated above or below the other. In the first theme, A is on top and B below: for the second the positions are reversed.

This leads to some confusion in the mind of the listener until
the personalities of the themes are very familiar. Possibly
Brahms did not consider this intrusion of polyphony entirely
successful himself for he does not repeat the scheme in the
other symphonies.

The second movements are all in song-form design. They
are lyric in style but difficult at first to follow, so subtle is the
arrangement of phrase. For the last movements, sonata-form
of extended proportions is the rule with the exception of the
Fourth Symphony which consists of a great passacaglia, built
somewhat on the lines of the Bach work we have studied, but
containing no fugue at the end and appearing to have a middle section where, although the regular restatement of the
theme continues, the treatment is more lyric. The essence of
the underlying theme is harmonic, the rhythm being regular
and the melody chiefly an upward scale.

Brahms, like Beethoven, uses unification of movements
sparingly. There is no example of such categorical restatement as we find in the introduction of the last movement of
the Ninth Symphony of Beethoven. However, we do find examples of great eloquence such as the reappearance of the
first movement principal theme in the violins at the very end
of the last movement of the Third Symphony, and the suggestion of theme A of the first movement in the second
phrase of the second movement of the First Symphony. As a
rule, Brahms is content to build each movement upon different material, achieving his unity in more subtle ways.

We have already discussed the great emphasis laid upon
cyclic treatment of themes by César Franck (1822–1890) and
his school. Franck, like Brahms, was a master of form and

entirely independent of his contemporaries. Although he wrote only one symphony, his sonata for violin and piano, quintet for piano and strings and string quartet are very fine examples of symphonic writing. Aside from the tendency to theme unification, we notice that he is quite polyphonic in style, being especially fond of canon and fugue and of theme combination. The logic of his developments is excellent, although less dramatic than Beethoven and less lyric than Brahms. He has a genius for symphonic themes which are both melodious and suitable for development.

If there is a serious weakness in the music of Franck it is his over-fondness for the chromatic scale and too frequent modulation. This sometimes gives his works a tonal instability, the modulation also leading him into sequences which somewhat lessen the musical interest. However, if any composer ever triumphed through high idealism, courage and an intellectual grasp of the problems of music, it was Franck who, even up to the time of his death, received practically no encouragement from the frivolous-minded musicians and public of Paris. That he was no slavish imitator of his divinity, Beethoven, is shown by certain of his formal innovations: in the first movement of the quartet which is sonata-form contained in a greatly expanded song-form, or in the violin sonata where not one of the four movements resembles the conventional arrangement. In his symphony, he combines the slow movement and scherzo in expanded ABA form; themes from both are combined to form the last section. Today the once-scorned D minor Symphony of Franck vies in popularity with the great Fifth Symphony of Beethoven.

Other frequently heard symphonies are the Fourth, Fifth

and Sixth of Tschaikowsky and the *New World* Symphony of Dvořák. Tschaikowsky (1840–1893) like Schubert is not a master of symphonic development but wins his popularity by wealth of melody. To this is added a reflection of his intense emotional nature and a dash of the fresh color of the Russian folk song to make his work interesting. His first movements are generally very long and rather loosely made. However, they are magnificently scored and sound as well, orchestrally speaking, as any symphonies in the literature.

The *New World* Symphony of Dvořák, which is supposed to be of especial interest to Americans because it is based upon folk material collected by Dvořák in this country, is much more Bohemian than American despite its origin. As music it is tuneful, especially in the second movement, the popular *Largo*. Dvořák (1841–1904) had a good sense of form, and the proportions of the symphony as well as its scoring are well calculated to protect it from time's ravages. In the matter of development it is much less fortunate, most of the working-out section being rather futile sequences of fragments of themes in the manner of Haydn. Although it pleases our ears, its melodies seem to wear out rather quickly, and at no time in the course of its long unfolding does it touch us very deeply.

Bruckner and Mahler, the German successors of Brahms, have never won any great degree of popularity in this country. Each wrote nine symphonies. Bruckner (1824–1896) was in reality a contemporary of Brahms, having been born some years before him. His symphonies show the influence of Wagner in musical subject matter and are extremely long and diffuse. Passages of great beauty alternate with music either derivative or dull.

Mahler (1860–1911) was obsessed by the desire to be as great as Beethoven and filled up tremendous symphonic canvases with music on a large scale. In addition to a huge orchestra, he sometimes calls for chorus or even solo soprano voice. Like Bruckner, he is somewhat defeated by lack of originality and pretentiousness. Although both composers have many devoted adherents, especially in Germany, their symphonies have yet to win a place in the standard orchestral repertory.

Among contemporary composers Sibelius (born 1865) has achieved outstanding success with his symphonies. At the present writing he has published seven symphonies and they appear with increasing frequency on concert programs. In these works we note many experiments with traditional form, orchestration of great originality and power, and a strong dramatic sense. The Fourth Symphony, almost bare in its outlines, cold and gray in color, is regarded by his admirers as his most typical work although not by far the most effective with audiences. Other twentieth-century composers of the symphony are D'Indy and Roussel in France, Elgar, Vaughan Williams and Arnold Bax in England, Rachmaninoff in Russia and in this country such contemporary figures as Daniel Gregory Mason, Edward Burlinghame Hill, David Stanley Smith, Howard Hanson, Randall Thompson, and Roger Sessions. No important changes have come from any of this group, the form still resting upon the symphonic style as exemplified by Brahms and Franck.

CHAPTER XV

The Symphonic Poem and Symphonic Suite

THE great change which came about in the composer's attitude toward his art at the beginning of the nineteenth century is well illustrated by Beethoven. Instead of conceiving music as objective design, as the classic masters did, composers of the romantic period became increasingly interested in its possibilities as a vehicle for the expression of ideas and emotions.

Not that the greatest composers of the nineteenth century advocated the abandonment of form for program, since each one of them insisted upon the limitations of music in pictorial descriptions. In speaking of his *Pastoral* Symphony Beethoven expressed the general attitude toward program music: "More the expression of inner feeling than picturing." The *Pastoral* Symphony itself shows little deviation from standard shape, the principal innovation being the inclusion of a fifth movement, portraying a storm in the country, between the scherzo and the finale.

Although the importance of design was always admitted, it was perfectly natural that a slight weakening of formal texture should ensue. Beethoven himself, master of form, permitted his interest in the expressive side of music to alter forms but, as we have seen, the resulting new forms suffered no loss of logic or of musical character.

Beethoven's successors and contemporaries, with the exception of Brahms and Wagner, had less genius than he for the conception and execution of new forms. Deviation from accepted designs generally brought with it a certain weakness and ambiguity. We find that up to the time of Brahms, the symphony suffered a decline. When composers such as Schubert, Schumann and Chopin wrote in sonata-form, it proved to be a less effective medium than others for their melodic and expressive gifts, with the result that they inclined to designs which imposed less formal obligations upon them. In writing for the piano, song-form and the single piece became the vogue instead of the sonata. These compositions of Schubert, Schumann and Chopin, so familiar on recital programs, should offer little difficulty to the listener.

In orchestral music, however, the short or extended song-form did not seem to provide a sufficiently large canvas. Accordingly, before Liszt, we find the romantic composers still writing overtures and symphonies, compositions of somewhat weakened design which gave an increasing importance to descriptive titles and emotional content. However, even Berlioz (1805–1869), who is generally regarded as the greatest enemy of absolute music, used the forms of the symphony more or less as employed by Beethoven in his orchestral compositions. The *Fantastic Symphony* for all its weird program is entirely explicable in terms of design alone. The reason why this symphony is less great than the symphonies of Beethoven is not that it is revolutionary in form, or relies too much upon poetical ideas; it is simply that the music is inferior to Beethoven's.

It was Liszt (1811–1886), master pianist and generous

friend to everything that was new in the art, who hit upon the form which came to be known as the *symphonic poem*. Liszt included in his manifold activities tours as piano virtuoso, teaching, producing of the meritorious works of other composers and conducting. In spite of these many occupations he found time to write thirteen symphonic poems and two symphonies.

Even Liszt, who succeeded in modifying classical form to this extent, fully realized the importance of definite form. He said in explaining his work: "Nobody thinks of writing music so ridiculous as that which they call picturesque. What one thinks of . . . is to impress music more and more with poetry in order to render it the organ of that part of the soul, which, if one may believe those who have felt, loved and suffered strongly, defies analysis and does not admit of the settled and definite expression of the human languages."

He continues: "The program has no other object than to indicate preparatively the spiritual movements which impelled the composer to create his work, the thoughts which he endeavored to incorporate in it." "In program music, the return, change, modification and modulation of the motives are conditioned by their relation to a poetic idea. All exclusively musical considerations, though they should not be neglected, have to be subordinated to the action of a given subject."

The symphonic poem, as exemplified in the works of Liszt, consists of one long movement easily divisible into sections. There may occur any number of changes of time and of key, and the composition may be based upon a number of themes. Unity is secured by plan of tonality, always well calculated in Liszt's works, repetition and development of themes. One feature of this development is called *theme metamorphosis*. It consists of presenting a theme in successively different shapes, bearing always a recognizable relationship to its original state but undergoing changes of rhythm, melody and harmony which give it an entirely different aspect. This theme metamorphosis is not unlike Beethoven's theme amplification. We find it not only in the symphonic poems of composers who come after Liszt, but even in the symphonies of Brahms.

It would seem that this somewhat loose form would be difficult to follow. It does not permit of standardization as we find it in other symphonic forms. Apart from the program there is no way of predicting what will occur in the composition. For this reason, in listening to a symphonic poem, our enjoyment is always enhanced by a previous understanding of the program, which generally suggests the division of the music into sections and even the disposition of themes.

Let us examine the symphonic poem of Liszt most often played, *Les Preludes*. The following program is given at the beginning of the composition, a prose selection from Lamartine: "What else is our life but a series of preludes to that unknown Hymn, the first and solemn note of which is intoned by Death?—Love is the glowing dawn of all existence; but where is the fate in which the first delights of happiness are not interrupted by some storm, the mortal blast of which dissipates its fine illusions, the fatal lightning of which consumes its altar; and where is the cruelly wounded soul which, on issuing from one of these tempests, does not endeavor to rest his recollection in the calm serenity of life in the fields? Nevertheless man hardly gives himself up for long to the enjoyment of the beneficent stillness which at first he has shared in Nature's bosom, and when 'the trumpet sounds the alarm,' he hastens to the dangerous post, whatever the war may be which calls him to its ranks, in order at last to recover in the combat full consciousness of himself and entire possession of his energy."

In considering this program a number of sections are obviously suggested. There will be a prelude, a section devoted to love, one to storm, one to pastoral music, one to battle and victory. These sections are easy to find in the Liszt composition. Program notes are usually furnished to those about to hear the composition and audiences have proved by their continued fondness for the piece that they follow its development with ease.

The musical design of *Les Preludes* partially resembles a theme and variations in twelve sections. Here is the musical plan:

1. Theme A in C major stated rather incompletely, *andante*.
2. A in C major fully presented, triumphant, *andante maestoso*.
3. A altered melodically presented first in C and then in E, suggestive of the love episode, very lyric.
4. Metamorphosis or amplification of melodic framework of A into a new and very lush melody in E major.
5. Modulatory passage ends in stating A in A minor.
6. The storm, based upon A, *allegro ma non troppo*.
7. A expressively stated in B flat major.

8. New pastoral theme introduced in A major, *allegretto*.
9. A as metamorphosed in section 4 is combined with the new pastoral theme in A major.
10. Climax of same material in C major.
11. Military theme derived from A in C major, *allegro marziale animato*.
12. A, triumphant, resembling section 2.

It will be seen that this form is really unlike any design we have studied before and that without its program it could not be satisfactorily explained. By its repetition and development, however, of a principal theme with contrasting material, it satisfies our instinct for symmetry. The music although somewhat bombastic in spots is very melodious and is effectively scored. Certainly Liszt has succeeded in what he set out to do. We may not care to be bothered with reading a long and rather perfervid program, but with its assistance we are never at a loss as to the composer's intentions or scheme of development.

Liszt's younger contemporary Saint-Saëns (1835–1921), the French composer, was much interested in the symphonic poem as a medium of composition. He wrote a number of these pieces, many of which are still played, particularly the popular *Danse Macabre*. Saint-Saëns, however, before embarking upon the symphonic poem had thorough training in symphonic style and his compositions are easily explained in terms of music alone. The *Danse Macabre,* for instance, is simply extended song-form presenting two themes in the same key in the first section, developing them for the middle part and restating them in the third section.

The most interesting figure in the symphonic poem after Liszt, and the composer who has done most to popularize the form, is Richard Strauss. Born in 1864, Strauss is still living and still writing. Of late years, however, he has been more interested in opera than in orchestral music, and his compositions which are most often played were written at the end of the nineteenth century.

Strauss based his symphonic poems upon the Liszt model, but brought to it a thorough knowledge of symphonic structure and an almost perfect technical equipment. In fact Strauss is so much a master of the orchestra, of polyphonic writing and theme manipulation that he blinds us to the mediocrity sometimes lurking beneath his complicated musical surfaces. Some of his symphonic poems, however, such as *Till Eulenspiegel, Don Juan, Death and Transfiguration, Ein Heldenleben* and *Don Quixote,* have taken their place in the standard repertory of the orchestra of today.

Strauss is less dependent upon his program than Liszt. The music often takes shapes which are readily explicable in forms as employed by Beethoven. Strauss has said himself, "The program is a poetical help in creating new shapes." These new shapes are, for the most part, not especially revolutionary developments of such familiar forms as theme and variations, rondo or even sonata-form.

Death and Transfiguration, one of the most compact of his works, is a good example to study. For the program, refer to Chapter One. As in the Liszt composition, it suggests an obvious plan of division into sections. There are six main parts of the work: a prelude describing the room and scene, recollection of boyhood, struggle with fate, love, death and transfiguration. The design in general resembles sonata-form. There is an introduction in which the two principal themes are sketched; following this is an *allegro, molto agitato,* given over to theme A in C minor. This leads to G major where theme B is stated. This is followed by a section given over to development of the two themes in various keys, in which the second theme is metamorphosed in such a way as to suggest the transfiguration theme to follow. The development ends with a great climax to indicate the death. The final section is given over to the altered second theme which rises to a great climax to end the work. Although the disposition of themes, providing for the omission of the first theme in the recapitulation-section, is not traditional and the first theme lacks clarity, the employment of keys and general proportions strongly suggest sonata-form as the basic scheme. At any rate, with the program available, we do not experience any difficulty in following the work. It would be an interesting experiment to study it without revealing the title or program and see how clear the effect would be.

Other more or less popular composers of symphonic poems are Tschaikowsky (1840–1893) who was admittedly programmatic even in his symphonies, but who wrote several symphonic poems, among them *Francesca da Rimini;* Scriabin the Russian composer of the early twentieth century whose symphonies are really symphonic poems in one movement; Debussy (1862–1918) whose *Afternoon of a Faun* is a masterpiece of design as well as an excellent bit of tone-painting; and certain other composers still living, Sibelius with the popular *Finlandia,* Ravel with *La Valse,* Dukas with *The Sorcerer's Apprentice* and Honegger with *Pacific 231.*

The tendency among contemporary composers of the symphonic poem is toward less program and more independence of design. Debussy, Ravel and Honegger have no story attached to their compositions; the title alone indicates that the material is influenced by a poetic idea. Among American composers of the symphonic poem are to be noted Ernest Schelling with *A Victory Ball,* Gershwin with *An American in Paris,* Hanson with *Pan and the Priest* and Sowerby with *Prairie.* The symphonic poem as conceived by Liszt is not in accord with the tendency of this age, being rather too diffuse and pretentious, but the idea of a symphonic composition in a single movement with descriptive title continues to be popular with both composers and audiences.

·　·　·　·　·　·　·　·　·

The orchestral suite, so frequently played at symphony concerts, is of two varieties. Neither one is to be confused with the eighteenth-century suite of Bach, Handel and their contemporaries. The old form of the suite has completely failed to interest composers since the time of Haydn. Examples of it in modern times might be found, but not among the works most familiar to audiences.

The first type consists of an arrangement of excerpts from incidental dramatic music or ballet. Although these excerpts may be in any form, they are generally in the simple design of the three-part song-form. The usual explanation of their collection and performance as a group of pieces apart from the stage work for which they were composed is that in this way successful dramatic music may be made available for the large concert-going public. Familiar examples of this type of suite are to be found in the *Nutcracker Suite* from a ballet of Tschaikowsky, the suite from *Peer Gynt* of Grieg, consisting of incidental music written for a performance of the Ibsen play, two suites from *L'Arlesienne* of Bizet originally intended to accompany the action of a play of Daudet, and a suite made by Stravinsky from his ballet *Petrouchka*.

The other type of suite is more interesting symphonically speaking, for instead of being an arbitrary arrangement of musical excerpts for concert performance, it is conceived as a suite entirely apart from dramatic representation. Usually it has a descriptive title like the symphonic poem, but differs from it in that it consists of a number of short movements. As in the symphonic poem, no definite form is prescribed but simple song-form is generally employed.

One of the best compositions of this type is the popular symphonic suite, *Scheherazade* of Rimsky-Korsakoff (1844–1909). This suite deals with four Arabian Nights stories and uses the background of the situation for an interesting cyclic treatment of themes. The first movement begins with a peremptory theme probably intended to represent the sultan. It is succeeded by a very elaborate melody played on a solo violin, doubtless Scheherazade. After the introduction of the themes a development of the first one forms the main body of the movement interlarded with suggestions of the second. The story is supposed to be that of Sinbad the Sailor. It is well suggested by the skilfully contrived rhythms of the composer which, aided by orchestration of unsurpassed excellence, produces one of the most effective sea pieces in existence. Rimsky uses the two protagonists and the sea as a point of departure, but from there on musical values come first. The piece is completely understandable as music without the aid of any program. Notice particularly the variations of the Scheherazade theme which occur in every movement.

The second movement is entitled *The Tale of the Prince Kalender*. It commences with the theme of Scheherazade as an introduction, again played upon solo violin, conveying the idea of the program. A new theme is introduced and developed with that of the story teller. It is interrupted by a trumpet call somewhat suggestive of the sultan's theme. A middle section follows, based upon this idea, and the piece concludes with a repetition of the first material.

The third movement, *The Young Prince and the Young Princess,* varies the scheme by omitting Scheherazade's theme at the beginning and starting right out with new material. This is also in ABA form with a new theme in the middle. The familiar violin figure appears in the last section.

The last movement suggests at the start that a crisis has arisen for the poor lady. The sultan's theme is stated in angry fashion and that of Scheherazade replies with great elaboration. A new theme is introduced suggesting the title of the movement, *Fête at Bagdad*. There is a second section in which one of the themes from the third movement appears, followed by development of the two principal themes. The fourth section again states the material from the third movement, and the fifth appropriately contains the fête music again. There is an important coda in which the sultan and his entertainer are suggested, and the triumph of Scheherazade, supposedly with her release, is indicated by the fine climax of the music based on a restatement of the sea music of the first movement.

It will be seen that this scheme of Rimsky-Korsakoff really does what Strauss recommended, allowing the program to suggest new forms. This suite is compactly and symphonically made. It creates forms for itself, but forms which are perfectly understandable as design alone. It also serves as a very ingenious illustration of the Arabian Nights story.

There are three symphonic suites of Tschaikowsky without descriptive titles, but they are not played so often as his more programmatic works and his symphonies. The most frequently heard symphonic suites in addition to *Scheherazade* are *Impressions of Italy* of Charpentier, *Caucasian Sketches* of Ippolitov-Ivanov, and the *Mother Goose Suite* of Ravel, originally written for piano duet but scored for orchestra by the composer.

Debussy (1862–1918), the great French composer, has three orchestral works of considerable popularity which might be classed as symphonic suites. *La Mer,* which he calls "symphonic sketches," *Iberia,* classified as "images," and the three *Nocturnes.* All of these consist of three separate movements, but particularly in the first two you will notice that the style is symphonic, a continuous development of thematic fragments against a changing background of orchestral color. Debussy's popularity today seems destined to last. His compositions are the work of a skilled and subtle artist, and the poetical ideas which he so beautifully incorporates in them are never permitted to interfere with the solidity of the musical design.

American composers have written a number of compositions in this style, several of them attaining considerable success. The *Indian Suite* of MacDowell, *Through the Look-*

ing Glass of Deems Taylor, and *Adventures in a Perambulator* of John Alden Carpenter are familiar to wide audiences. Arthur Shepherd has written a suite, *Horizons,* which in addition to the use in one of the movements of American cowboy tunes has a native flavor to recommend it. Jazz has been effectively employed by Gruenberg in his *Jazz Suite* and by Copland in his *Music for the Theatre.*

The suite as a rule is easier to follow than the symphonic poem because its movements are relatively short and usually in simple song-form. Well-balanced orchestral programs usually contain a serious work, like a symphony, followed or preceded by lighter pieces, such as overtures, symphonic poems, suites and short pieces.

CHAPTER XVI

Opera and Oratorio, etc.

THERE are a number of important considerations which enter into the relationship of words and music. To begin with, words when sung or spoken are sounds in themselves; when combined with music they are contributory to the resultant effect. The composer of a song or an opera takes into consideration the sound of the words which he uses; they are frequently important to the effectiveness of the music. This is shown by examining certain translations of operatic texts. In the scene from *Die Walküre* when Fricka scolds Wotan for his philanderings the music is heightened by the explosive quality of the original German text. Translated into French as sung at the Paris Opera, Fricka's music becomes definitely less abusive, the caressing sounds of the French words considerably diminishing the original quality of the music. On the other hand when the *Toreador Song* is translated into German, it loses much of its Gallic suavity. Compare "Toreador hab' acht" with "Toreador prends garde" for sound. When we add to the falsification of sound values which translation of text produces, the fact that the translated text must parallel the meter of the original syllable for syllable in order to accommodate the music, and as a result is usually unspeakably silly, it is hard to make out a case for opera in the ver-

nacular. Naturally it is important that the audience understand the play, but must this be accomplished at such cost to
musical and poetic values? American audiences are fortunate
in that they usually have a chance to hear operas with the
original texts, but opera-going when seriously undertaken by
the American requires more preparation than by the European, who is accustomed to hearing the text in his own language and to following without effort.

Even aside from the difficulties attendant upon translating
word-music from one language to another, musical language
and word-language really occupy different realms and have
different purposes. Word-language aims first of all at exact-
ness of communication and only secondarily at sensuous
sound. Music-language is first of all interested in pattern of
sound and has only limited interest and ability in the communication of ideas. The union of these two languages, therefore, brings about a conflict of cross-purposes.

Furthermore, word-language and music-language have by
no means the same ideas of design. Repeated refrains are
sometimes found in verse but as a rule repetition of word or
phrase is not greatly admired in verse or prose. In music, as
we have seen, repetition is essential to solidity of design.
Whenever words and music are combined there is a clash of
interests; one element or the other must be subordinated.
Speaking and singing represent separate spheres; speaking
does not combine successfully with music, and singing places
obvious handicaps in the way of simple communication of
an idea. We have seen this irreconcilability in the strophic
song. In the opera we shall find it an ever present problem,
one never yet satisfactorily solved in the history of the art.

The scope of the present volume does not admit of a detailed description of the development of opera, yet while we are mainly concerned with design as exemplified in the great operatic masterpieces, the history of opera as in the case of the symphony explains much that might otherwise seem needlessly complicated.

Opera started about 1600 in the attempt by some Florentine noblemen to revive the ancient music drama of the Greeks. It was believed that if the relationship which history tells us existed in Greek art could be rediscovered, dramatic values could be enhanced by the expressive quality of the music. None of the forms then in use was satisfactory for such an experiment, so the opera composers struck out boldly and produced a new form, a sort of musical speech, allowing the voice to follow closely the accents of language but employing musical tone. This declamatory song is called *recitative*. Its musical value is slight because it is so completely dominated by the words. The first operas were continuous recitatives and must have been very tedious; to make them more interesting, composers gradually added set musical pieces such as songs for solo performers, duets, trios, etc., or chorus pieces. Even as early as Monteverdi, whose operas came shortly after the first experiments, interpolated music varied the effect of the otherwise continuous recitative.

Once the public had a chance to hear arias and concerted pieces, the sovereignty of the drama was at an end. Recitative declined in importance until only as much as was needed to explain the plot was included, and the opera became a group of unrelated musical pieces. In the time of Handel, singers were the main consideration so that even musical values suffered. Opera plots had to be so arranged that the principal singers had an equal amount to do and sang in regular rotation. Also the arias had to be so constructed as to display the vocal technique of the artist. As a result the plots became purely perfunctory and were written by the merest hacks.

The great reformation of Gluck (1714–1787) consisted in relegating the singers to their proper position, building up recitative so as to be expressive and musical, and lessening emphasis in design of the solos and ensembles. He chose very simple plots without a great deal of action and in this way was able to unify the effect. To us today, Gluck's operas seem very old-fashioned because the recitative and musical piece are still very sharply defined; but in his own time his artistic sincerity and lack of showiness brought about a great operatic war between his partisans and his enemies.

Mozart, whose operas are as great as his symphonies, was not a reformer at all, accepting the current fashions without question. But although he endowed them with tremendous vitality, his operas have survived rather because of their superlative melodies, than because of their dramatic importance. As dramatic spectacles they seem very silly, particularly *The Magic Flute* which is a strong competitor for the world's worst libretto. We do notice, however, that although Mozart invariably uses recitatives followed by set pieces, he is able to achieve much characterization in his music. It is in this feature of opera that he is interesting from the dramatic point of view.

Other late eighteenth-century and early nineteenth-century composers, such as Rossini, Bellini, Donizetti among the Italians, and Weber and Meyerbeer among the Germans, wrote the same type of opera as Mozart. In fact this is the universal form of opera, exceptions proving the rule. These composers varied greatly in their treatment of the recitative, the chorus and soloists and the orchestra, but you will find that their operas are all made in the same shape. Verdi, the great Italian who lived for so many years and belongs to more than one age of music, in his early operas followed the paths of his predecessors unquestioningly.

At this point Wagner (1813–1883) arrived upon the scene in the full flower of the romantic age, with the music of Beethoven, Schubert and Weber already established. He was of a different type from the usual operatic composer, anxious to lead rather than to follow the public taste, a man of tremendous intellectual power and high idealism. In him there existed a strong dramatic sense as well as one of the greatest musical gifts in history. His taste for the drama impelled him toward works for the stage; he deplored the ignoble state to which the operatic art had reduced the drama. His musical taste recognized in Beethoven the triumph of symphonic art, the only possible musical path for him to follow.

It would seem that these two tendencies in Wagner were irreconcilable. Perhaps they were, but if the music drama which he conceived was a failure, it was a glorious one which gave to the world some of its most highly prized music. His career shows the gradual clarification of purpose and method. His early success, *Rienzi,* written in imitation of the popular Meyerbeer style, he later entirely repudiated. The next opera, *The Flying Dutchman,* showed a great advance in musical unification, he discovers the *leit-motiv,* he begins to lessen the gap between the recitative and the set piece so that the flow of the music will be continuous. From this point on through *Tannhäuser* and *Lohengrin* and the first two operas of the *Nibelungen Ring* he is building up his style until in *Tristan and Isolda* he arrives at the perfect (to him) embodiment of his theories. From this point on with the exception of *The Mastersingers* which was conceived as a comic opera, and which sometimes reverts to the earlier style, his operas are entirely distinct from anything which precedes them; sustained musical compositions, completely unified and with no apparent divisions within the acts.

Wagner was not at all reticent in discussing himself or his theories so we have excellent records of his ideas. The principal theories which are seen to be embodied in his mature works are:

1. The use of the myth as a subject because of its impersonality and its generally heroic character.

2. Union of the arts in the music-drama. He wrote his own librettos and considered them just as important as the music. He also supervised all details of scenery and production.

3. The use of the orchestra as the principal factor rather than the singer. In this way he was able to free his music from the domination of words, but by the use of subsidiary declamatory music superimposed upon the orchestral web, he was able to preserve the integrity of diction and of the dramatic values.

4. Unification by means of the *leit-motiv,* called *tone speech.* This consisted of short concentrated musical ideas to be associated with characters and abstract ideas so that their restatement would convey a meaning to the audience.

Wagner was enormously successful in his employment of tone speech. Opera-goers who take the trouble to prepare in advance by familiarizing themselves with the motives and their significance are able to follow the action without understanding a word of the libretto. The most magnificent effect is achieved in the Funeral March of Siegfried in *The Dusk of the Gods* where he gives us not only a moving death march, but also reviews Siegfried's life and ancestry by the succession of motives employed.

But the most significant thing about the mature operas of Wagner is one which he stresses somewhat less than the others. It is their symphonic aspect. Deeply devoted to Beethoven, he studied the symphonies so that he absorbed many features of Beethoven's style. He was particularly interested in musical development, theme amplification and the search for unending melody as exemplified in Beethoven's last works. Wagner believed that Beethoven, by including Schiller's *Ode to Joy* in the Ninth Symphony, practically admitted that instrumental music was incapable of further expansion without fertilization by poetry. Accordingly he felt that in his music drama he was carrying on the symphonic art as the true successor of Beethoven; and indeed it must be admitted that the operas are not operas in the true sense, but extended tone poems for orchestra with vocal embellishments.

In listening to the Wagner operas, it is of the greatest importance to recognize the musical subject matter, for they are nothing but extended developments of a number of themes. In addition to serving as tone speech for dramatic purposes, the *leit-motivs* are symphonic themes upon which successive scenes of the operas are built. It would be impossible to follow the forms used in the course of the musical unfolding although often suggestions of traditional symphonic designs are to be found. Here, however, concentration upon subject matter and recognition of its development is the main musical pleasure to be obtained. The Wagner operas are excellent to study as preparation for the more concentrated developments of themes to be found in the symphony.

The general plan of *Tristan and Isolda* is a succession of scenes without pause, constituting an act. In each one of the scenes a new important theme is introduced which serves, with the assistance of repetitions of previous important themes, as the basis for development. In this way the music is continuously freshened by the introduction of new material but is unified with what has gone before. Four of the principal themes of the opera are stated in the prelude. The very first notes you will hear constitute the most important theme in the work. If you familiarize yourself thoroughly with this and listen for it as the opera proceeds, you will be astonished that it can appear so many times without becoming tiresome.

The operas of Wagner have always attracted a different public from the usual opera. They require musicianship on the part of the audience, an understanding of material, or they will become very tedious in spite of their frequently stirring moments. No special musical sensitiveness is required to appreciate the other type of opera. The music all appears in short forms easily followed, and if even this slight musical concentration is not desired by the listener, there is always something to watch on the stage. Wagner realizes that the eye is a distraction to the ear so he usually manoeuvers his characters into stationary positions which can persist for as long a time as the music requires. The singers are made as comfortable as possible, you should be comfortable, relax, give up expecting anything to happen and listen to the music. People who prefer entertainment for the eye should studiously refrain from attending the Wagner operas.

Wagner's success was slow in coming for his art was very revolutionary. When it did come, however, it was overpowering. His influence was tremendous. Even the strongly intrenched Verdi felt the urge to add symphonic texture to his operas. In his last two compositions, *Othello* and *Falstaff,* although he does not employ the *leit-motiv* as a means of unification, the music is much more unified than before. Recitative and set piece are practically indistinguishable. Dramatic values are much more highly prized. This is true of most of the other late nineteenth-century opera composers, Gounod, Saint-Saëns and Massenet in France, Borodin and Moussorgsky in Russia and Puccini and others in Italy. Some of these composers used the *leit-motiv* idea without much success. Puccini, for instance, in the first act of *Madame Butterfly,* frequently uses the introductory theme which is supposed to be very Japanese, but the effect eventually becomes tiresome. He is really interested in the arias and duets which punctuate the score; symphonic development is not sympathetic to his nature. The same is true of Charpentier in *Louise.* You hear the theme supposed to identify the father in the first act so many times that it becomes unbearably tedious. Of course there are themes and themes and it would be unfair to expect Puccini and Charpentier to compete with Wagner in the manufacture of salient themes.

On the whole Wagner's method was peculiar to himself

and his symphonic gifts fitted him to employ it. Gradually opera is reverting to its traditional plan of recitative for plot and aria for music. The distinction between them will probably never be the same as it was before Wagner, but until another symphonic-minded composer prefers to write operas rather than symphonies, we shall probably have them based on the old form.

The only composer who has succeeded in suggesting another form is Debussy, who with *Pelléas and Mélisande* brought about a private revolution in France. At first a great admirer of Wagner, Debussy came to feel that his principles and musical idiom were stifling the true progress of music in France. Accordingly he wrote his single opera as a protest, and it was so received and acclaimed by youthfully minded people at the beginning of the twentieth century. The Debussy plan was somewhat like the Wagnerian one in that the music is chiefly in the orchestra and the voice parts are declamatory, also in the continuous flow of the music without employing the set piece. However, instead of concentrating his music symphonically by the development of *leit-motivs,* Debussy relies upon only three or four themes which appear from time to time in development; the main body of the score consists of an impressionistic music, descriptive of the stage action. In this way dramatic values are better preserved than in Wagner with his rather absurd stationary figures. In *Pelléas and Mélisande* the action is natural although poetically conceived. The opera seems as satisfactory dramatically as the original Maeterlinck play, in fact even more so because the music makes it infinitely more expressive. Perhaps it is Debussy who has captured the true relationship between the music and the drama of the Greeks, sought so many times in the history of opera.

. . . .

Oratorio, which is really opera with a sacred text presented in concert form, does not present all the problems of opera. Since the eye is not distracted by action, nor the singers by costumes and scenery, the attention is more concentrated upon musical values. The words still exert upon the music a powerful and by no means friendly influence, but if they are distorted by long figures of melody upon a single syllable, no one much cares, for here music is distinctly the thing. Accordingly we find that the oratorio generally consists of music of more symphonic design. Choruses are more polyphonic than in the opera, the aria is allowed to follow its natural desire for the ABA form. The nature of the text permits of music of a greater degree of seriousness and tragedy of a more moving nature.

The oratorio was made popular by Handel who, as manager of an opera house, hit upon it as a device to keep his company and theatre employed during Lent, at which time people were not inclined to visit the theatre. Its form has not changed to any degree since its origin. Many of the greatest composers have written in this category, among them Handel, Bach, Haydn, Mendelssohn and Franck. More recently successful oratorios have been written by Elgar, the American composer, Horatio Parker, and Stravinsky. The oratorios of Bach, the St. Matthew and St. John Passions, are among his greatest works. In the St. Matthew Passion which deals with the story of the trial and crucifixion of Jesus, Bach uses his chorus with striking dramatic effect. The characters of the drama are represented in recitative, there are frequent arias descriptive of exalted states of feeling, but the chorus represents the mob and the part it played in the story. It shouts for the release of Barabbas, for the execution of Jesus and again it weeps at his tomb. It also is used for simple four-part chorals which are interspersed throughout the action, but which are really intended to be sung by the audience.

    .   .   .   .

The *cantata* is a choral form. It originally consisted of a short drama in recitative without dramatic action and as such was written by many of the early Italian composers, among them Carissimi, Alessandro Scarlatti and Pergolesi.

Bach employed the form as a short religious service in his church at Leipzig. One type of the cantata is based upon a familiar German choral from which it takes its name. A polyphonic chorus begins the work, there are recitatives and arias and for the end a simple four-part harmonization of the choral. A beautiful example of the choral cantata is *Christ lag in Todesbanden* which is available in complete recording. Bach wrote five complete sets of cantatas, one for every Sunday and holiday of the year, but as in the case of his other choral works many of them have been lost. In those that remain to us we find some of his greatest music.

In modern times the cantata is usually a work for chorus set to a sacred text which is too short to be called an oratorio. A good example of modern cantata is Debussy's *Prodigal Son* with which he won the "Prix de Rome."

The other great branch of choral music concerns itself

directly with the Roman Catholic service, the *mass*. From earliest times of Christianity the service has included five musical parts each serving its particular function, the Kyrie Gloria, Credo, Sanctus, Benedictus and Agnus Dei. During the Middle Ages when unaccompanied monophonic music of the type known as Gregorian chant was used, many masses were composed and sung. Later when the great polyphonic school of Palestrina appeared, the mass was the principal form of composition. In Gregorian chant, design was little organized, the music following the lead of the words. In the Palestrinian mass, the form found in the motet was ordinarily the rule. Masses were usually based upon traditional Gregorian themes.

In the time of Bach, composers again became interested in the mass although the type of composition produced was rather too long for inclusion in the service. Bach's great B Minor Mass, written to the Catholic order of service although he himself was a devoted Protestant, is probably his greatest composition. It falls into the traditional parts, but each section of the words is made to contain a number of separate pieces. Some of these are for chorus and some are arias or duets as the language of the particular part seems to suggest. The Kyrie consists of three parts, the Gloria and Credo of eight, the Sanctus and Agnus Dei of two and the Benedictus of one.

One of the great advantages of the use of the text of the mass is that its words may be indefinitely divided and only one phrase used for a musical piece. The repetition of this phrase corresponds with the natural inclination of musical phrases to repeat themselves. In the Bach mass the choruses are polyphonic, some of them strict fugues and others using imitation in a somewhat freer form like the old motet. The arias contain lovely melodies and beautiful imitation between voice and instrumental accompaniment. There are no recitatives, another advantage of the mass musically speaking.

Since Bach many fine concert masses have been written, some of them as a special form, the Requiem mass for the dead, and others of the ordinary variety. Many musicians consider Mozart's Requiem Mass his finest work, as well as in the case of Beethoven, his Missa Solemnis. Both compositions were among the last works of their composers. The maturity of style added to the naturally elevating quality of the words brought about in both instances great inspiration.

Among other composers of the mass there is Berlioz with his tremendous Requiem, Brahms with his German Requiem in which instead of the usual words he employs a biblical text to produce one of his greatest works, and the French composer Fauré, who has written a very lovely Requiem Mass.

The mass is the last form that we shall study in our survey of musical forms. Although this study has been necessarily rapid and incomplete, enough has been provided to form the basis for further observation of music and musical form. The musical listener should not burden his mind with a collection of facts unrelated to actual experience. The best way to proceed in the acquisition of listening skill is to study works one at a time and master only those facts which seem pertinent to that particular work. In this way facts become an accessory to actual experience and are remembered with less effort.

At the risk of tedious insistence, let us again assert that it is from musical experience that knowledge of music is gained. Books about music are interesting only if the music which they explain has made them so.

APPENDIX

CHAPTER I

Exercise 1. Examine the following records which are descriptive and note the musical effects which seem to have any bearing on the story. For an explanation of the material upon which they are based consult Rosa Newmarch, *Concert-goer's Library of Descriptive Notes* (Oxford Press) and Elson, *Standard Concert Guide* (McClure).

> Beethoven, *Pastoral Symphony No. 6,* 3rd movement, Thunderstorm
> Dukas, *The Sorcerer's Apprentice*
> Liszt, *Mazeppa*
> Moussorgsky, *A Night on the Bald Mountain*
> Rimsky-Korsakoff, *Flight of the Bumble Bee*
> Strauss, *Don Quixote*
> Stravinsky, *Petrouchka*
> Berlioz, *Fantastic Symphony*
> Honegger, *Pacific 231*
> Tschaikowsky, *Overture of 1812*
> Wagner, *Siegfried's Rhine Journey*
> Ravel, *Mother Goose*

Exercise 2. Select the following records and play them at random without looking at the title which in each case is indicative of the expressive content of the music. Note your own impressions in each case and compare them with the expressed intent of the music.

Chabrier, *Joyous March*
Debussy, *Festivals* from *Three Nocturnes*
Dvořák, *Indian Lament*
Franck, *Heroic Piece* (for organ)
Liszt, *A Dream of Love*
Schumann, *Pleading Child* from *Scenes from Childhood*
Tschaikowsky, *Pathetic Symphony,* 4th movement, *adagio lamentoso*
Wagner, *Good Friday Spell* from *Parsifal*
　　　　　Love Death from *Tristan and Isolda*
Scriabin, *Poem of Ecstasy*

CHAPTER II

Exercise 1. Experiment at the piano in identifying the tones that you hear, either natural sounds, or notes played on other instruments. See if you can sing a tone which cannot be found on the piano and identify its nearest neighbor that you can find.

Exercise 2. Familiarize yourself with the names of the notes of the scale and their locations on the piano keyboard. Try the effect of the ancient modes instead of the C major scale. These consist of the series of white notes on D, E, F, G, and A.

Exercise 3. Experiment with glasses and a pitcher of water. The tone will be lower as you add water. See if you can tune several into the relationship of the first five notes of the scale.

Exercise 4. Examine examples of oriental music which you will find in the German Album, *Musik des Orients,* edited by Kurt Sachs (Parlaphone). Notice the use of tones outside our system.

Suggestions for further reading on Chapter 2:
Pole, *The Philosophy of Music,* Chapter 1, Harcourt Brace

APPENDIX 279

CHAPTER III

Exercise 1. Examine the *Instruments of the Orchestra*, charts and records published by the Victor Company. Learn to identify the instruments by sight and by sound.

Exercise 2. Examine the following records for characteristic solos of the principal orchestral instruments:

Piccolo—*Caucasian Sketches, Procession of the Czardas*, Ippolitov-Ivanov

Flute—*The Afternoon of a Faun*, Debussy

Oboe—Introduction to *Samson and Delilah*, Saint-Saëns

Clarinet—*Clarinet Quintet*, Mozart

English Horn—*Symphony in D minor*, 2nd movement, Franck

Bassoon—*The Sorcerer's Apprentice*, Dukas

Horn—*Fifth Symphony*, 2nd movement, Tschaikowsky

Trumpet—*Life of a Hero*, Strauss

Trombone—*Ride of the Valkyries*, Wagner

Tuba—Overture to *The Rhinegold*, Wagner

Harp—*Waltz of the Flowers* from *Nutcracker Suite*, Tschaikowsky

Violin—*Concerto in E minor* for violin and orchestra, Mendelssohn

Viola—*Trio in E flat major* for viola, clarinet and piano, Mozart

Cello—*Concerto for violin, cello and orchestra*, 1st movement, Brahms

Bass—*Fifth Symphony, Scherzo*, second part, Beethoven

Exercise 3. Examine the following records for characteristic orchestral combination of instruments:

Tschaikowsky, *Fourth Symphony, Scherzo*

  Pizzicato strings, followed by wood wind, followed by brass

Debussy, *Festivals*—middle section

  Solo, muted trumpets—accompaniment, string pizzicato, harps

  Solo, full wood winds—accompaniment, strings

  Solo, trombones—accompaniment, strings, horns, wood-winds

Rimsky-Korsakoff, *Scheherazade, The Young Prince and the Young Princess*

Weber, *Overture* to *Der Freischutz*—Introduction

  Solo horns accompanied by strings

Strauss, *Till Eulenspiegel's Merry Pranks*—beginning

  Strings and wood wind

  Solo horn—accompaniment, strings

  Solo oboes—accompaniment, strings

  Solo clarinets—accompaniment, strings

  Solo bassoons—accompaniment, strings

  Full orchestra

Exercise 4. Compare the recordings of these compositions and indicated transcriptions. Note the effects which are different because of the different instrumental medium.

	Original	Transcription
Bach, *Italian Concerto*	Harpsichord	Piano
Little G minor Fugue	Organ	Orchestra
French Suite in G, Gavotte	Clavichord	Piano
Chopin, *Nocturne in E flat*	Piano	Violin

Suggestions for further reading:

 Mason, *Orchestral Instruments and What They Do,* H. W. Gray

Forsyth, *Orchestration,* Macmillan (For reference, giving
   compass, etc.)

CHAPTER IV

Exercise 1. Analyse the following folk tunes noting meter,
phrase division, length of phrase, anacrusis, and phrase endings.

> *Annie Laurie*
> *Carry Me Back to Old Virginny*
> *The British Grenadiers*
> *Juanita*
> *The Minstrel Boy*
> *Drink To Me Only With Thine Eyes*

Exercise 2. Examine the following records for characteristic
meters.

> *Examples of 2/4 meter:*
>   Beethoven, *Seventh Symphony,* 2nd movement
>   *Fifth Symphony,* 1st movement
>   Haydn, *Surprise Symphony,* 2nd movement
>
> *Examples of 3/4 meter:*
>   Beethoven, *Fifth Symphony,* 2nd movement
>   Brahms, *First Symphony,* 2nd movement
>   Sibelius, *Valse Triste*
>
> *Examples of 4/4 meter:*
>   Wagner, Prelude to *The Mastersingers*
>   Tschaikowsky, *Pathetic Symphony,* 3rd movement
>
> *Examples of 6/8 meter:*
>   Beethoven, *Seventh Symphony, allegro* from 1st movement
>   Schubert, *Hark, Hark the Lark*
>
> *Example of 5/4 meter:*
>   Tschaikowsky, *Pathetic Symphony,* 2nd movement

Example of 9/8 meter:
> Bizet, *Carmen, Micaela's Air, I say that I am not faint-
> hearted*

Examples of 12/8 meter:
> Handel, *The Messiah, Pastoral Symphony*
> Chopin, *E flat Nocturne*

Suggestions for further reading:
> C. F. Addy Williams, *The Rhythm of Modern Music,* Mac-
> millan, London

CHAPTER V

Exercise 1. Using the keyboard design in Chapter 2, locate the
ascending and descending minor scale on A, the chromatic scale,
the major scale on G, B flat and E.

Exercise 2. Identify the degree of the scale used for each phrase
beginning and ending of the melodies listed for rhythmic analysis
in the last chapter. Compare their effect as to cadence.

Suggestions for further reading:
Parry, *The Evolution of Musical Art,* Appleton, Chapter on Scales

CHAPTER VI

Exercise 1. At the piano pick out the triads of the major scale
on C. Note those which are major and which minor. Pick out the
triads of the harmonic minor scale on A using the degrees A–B–
C–D–E–F–G sharp–A. Note which are major and which minor.

Exercise 2. Make a list from memory of the folk songs which you
know, that you believe to be based on a minor scale. Can you
think of a melody other than those cited in the text which uses
degrees from the chromatic scale?

Exercise 3. Examine the folk tunes listed under Chapter 4 for authentic and plagal cadences.

Exercise 4. Examine the following records and compare the degree of dissonance used in the harmony.

Palestrina, *Adoremus te Christe*
Haydn, *Surprise Symphony,* 2nd movement
Beethoven, *Moonlight Sonata,* 1st movement
Chopin, *Prelude in C minor*
Wagner, *Prelude* to *Tristan and Isolda*
Ravel, *Forlane* from *Le Tombeau de Couperin*
Stravinsky, *The Rites of Spring, Spring Rounds*

Exercise 5. Play combinations of two tones at the keyboard. Try to decide whether they are dissonant or consonant. If dissonant, try resolving them to consonances.

Suggestions for further reading:
Pole, *The Philosophy of Music*
Dyson, *The New Music,* Oxford Press (an interesting survey of the modern idiom)

CHAPTER VII

Exercise 1. Without playing the music analyse from memory the design of any folk song that you can recall.

Exercise 2. Analyse the design of the following compositions, noting general plan and pattern of phrases in each section.

Saint-Saëns, *The Swan*—pattern of similar phrases like *Träumerei*
Chopin, *Nocturne in G minor*—large ABA

Mozart, *Turkish March*—three principal sections each containing repetition, long added section to conclude

CHAPTER VIII

Exercise 1. Experiment at the piano with simple modulations. From keyboard chart locate fundamental triad of C major.

a) Add B flat to starting chord—follow by fundamental triad of F major.

b) Follow the C major triad by the triad on D, the second degree, change F to F sharp. Follow this by the fundamental triad of G major.

c) Follow the C major triad by the triad on E, the third degree. Change the G in this chord to G sharp. Follow by the fundamental triad of A major.

d) Change the E in the C major triad to E flat. Follow by the fundamental triad of E flat major.

In each case follow the modulating chord with the tonic chord of the new key and establish this by an authentic cadence in the new key. This can be obtained by playing the triad on the fifth degree of the new scale, succeeded by the tonic triad. For best results use the melody 1-7-1 and bass 1-5-1 (counting the degrees of the new scale).

CHAPTER IX

Exercise 1. Examine the following records for themes of outstanding rhythmic, melodic, or harmonic interest. (In the case of first movements of symphonies with slow introduction, the themes will appear at the beginning of the *allegro*. Other themes appear immediately.)

Rhythmic—Beethoven, *Second Symphony,* 1st theme, 1st movement

Mozart, *G minor Symphony,* 1st theme, 1st movement

Dvořák, *The New World Symphony,* 1st theme, 1st movement

Melodic—Brahms, *Second Symphony,* 1st theme, 1st movement

Schubert, *Unfinished Symphony,* 1st theme, 1st movement (In bass)

Tschaikowsky, *Pathetic Symphony,* 1st theme, 1st movement

Harmonic—Brahms, *Fourth Symphony,* 1st theme, 4th movement

Dvořák, *New World Symphony,* Introduction to 2nd movement

Wagner, *Prelude* to *Tristan and Isolda,* 1st motive, 2nd half.

Exercise 2. Examine the first theme from the first movement of the following symphonies and isolate any concentrated material which you think might serve as a motive. After you have done this, play the whole movement and see if you have selected the ones emphasized by the composer.

Mozart, *Jupiter Symphony* (C major)

Haydn, *London Symphony* (D major)

Beethoven, *First Symphony*

For further study of the motives from the Wagner operas see Lavignac, *The Music Dramas of Richard Wagner,* Dodd, Mead & Co. For records see 90 *Motives from the Ring,* played by the London Symphony.

CHAPTER X

Exercise 1. Examine the record of *O Magnum Mysterium* by Vittoria for polyphonic imitation. How many separate voices are there? What, in general, is their relation to each other? Are there any concentrated motives?

Exercise 2. Play the record of the *C major Fugue* from Vol. 1, *Well-Tempered Clavichord.* Discuss the musical personality of the subject. How many separate voices are there? What is their order of entrance? How many times does the full subject appear in the composition? Are there any special polyphonic devices used? Describe any that you hear.

CHAPTER XI

Exercise 1. Examine the first movement of Beethoven's Sonata, Opus 7. Isolate the themes and motives from the first section. Describe the musical character of each. Then play the development-section and note which themes are used and how each one is treated in development.

Exercise 2. Examine the first movement of the *New World Symphony* of Dvořák. Isolate the themes and motives from the first section. Describe each. Play the development-section and note which themes appear and the devices by which they are developed.

CHAPTER XII

Exercise 1. Examine the following records for illustration of early instrumental forms.

French Overture—Bach, *Suite in B minor,* 1st movement
Italian Overture—Mozart, *Overture* to *The Abduction from the Seraglio*
Fantasia—Bach, *Fantasia in G minor* for organ
Rondo—Haydn, *Quartet Opus 33 no. 3,* last movement
              Couperin, *Les Moissonneurs*
Minuet—Handel, *Minuet* from *Fireworks Music*

Variations—Corelli, *La Folia*
           Mozart, *Sonata for piano in A major,* 1st movement
Suite—Bach, *English Suite in A minor*
Concerto—Bach, *Concerto in D minor for 2 violins*
           Bach, *Brandenburg Concerto Number 2*

Supplementary reading:
For description of musical forms see *Grove's Dictionary,* Article
   on Form
For the History of Music, the following are recommended:
Nef, *An Outline of the History of Music,* Columbia Press
Pratt, *History of Music* (Convenient for reference), G. Schirmer
Bekker, *The Story of Music* (General reading), Norton
Dyson, *The Progress of Music* (Interesting survey), Oxford

CHAPTER XIII

Exercise 1. Examine the following compositions for details of
formal organization.

First movement sonata-form—Beethoven, *Quartet Opus 18, no 1*
           Mozart, *Symphony in E flat,* 1st
           movement

Exercise 2. Compare the following types of slow movement.
Sonata-form—Mozart, *Symphony in G minor,* 2nd movement
Song-form—Haydn, *London Symphony,* D major, 2nd movement
Theme and Variations—Haydn, *Surprise Symphony,* 2nd move-
   ment

Exercise 3. Compare the following minuets.
Type resembling suite in first part—Mozart, *Minuet* from *Sym-
   phony* in *G minor*
Type resembling song-form in first part—Haydn, *Minuet* from
   Surprise Symphony

Exercise 4. Compare the following types of finale.

Sonata-form—Mozart, *Symphony in C major* (*Jupiter*), last movement

Rondo-sonata—Haydn, *Surprise Symphony,* last movement

   Beethoven, *Sonata opus 13* for piano, last movement

Theme and Variations—Mozart, *Quartet no. 2* (Kochel 421), last movement

   Supplementary reading:

Mason, *Beethoven and His Forerunners,* Macmillan

Hussey, *Mozart,* Kegan Paul

Brenet, *Haydn,* Oxford Press

CHAPTER XIV

The following records are recommended for study and analysis:

Examples of sonata-form:
   Beethoven, *Third Symphony,* 1st movement
      Eighth Symphony, 1st movement
   Weber, *Overture to Euryanthe*
   Brahms, *Third Symphony,* 1st movement
   Schubert, *Symphony in C major,* 1st movement
   Mendelssohn, *Italian Symphony,* 1st movement

Examples of slow movement in song-form:
   Beethoven, *Fourth Symphony,* 2nd movement
   Brahms, *Third Symphony,* 2nd movement

Examples of slow movement in variation-form:
   Beethoven, *Fifth Symphony*
      Seventh Symphony

Example of scherzo (*Beethoven type*):
   Beethoven, *Ninth Symphony*

Example of scherzo linked to finale:
    Beethoven, *Fifth Symphony*, Scherzo and Finale

Example of Brahms 3rd movement type:
    Brahms, *Third Symphony*, 3rd movement

Examples of finale in sonata-form:
    Beethoven, *Seventh Symphony*, Finale
    Schubert, *C major Symphony*, Finale

Examples of finale in variation-form:
    Beethoven, *Third Symphony*, Finale
               Ninth Symphony, Finale (with chorus)
    Brahms, *Fourth Symphony*, Finale (Passacaglia)

Example of cyclic symphony:
    Franck, *Symphony in D minor* (entire)

Examples of Beethoven quartets:
    Quartet opus 18 no. 1, early style
    Quartet opus 131, late style

Example of late Beethoven sonatas:
    Sonata in A flat opus 110

Supplementary reading:
For further studies in analysis, the following are recommended:
Tovey, *Essays in Musical Analysis*, (2 vols.) Oxford Press
Upton, *The Standard Symphonies*, McClurg
Grove, *Beethoven and His Nine Symphonies*, Novello
Weingartner, *Symphony Writers Since Beethoven*, Reeve

For biographical material, the following are recommended:
Sullivan, *Beethoven*, Knopf
Kobald, *Franz Schubert and His Times*, Knopf
Hadow, *Studies in Modern Music*, 1st and 2nd series, Macmillan
Mason, *The Romantic Composers*, Macmillan

Fuller-Maitland, *Johannes Brahms,* Methuen
Modeste Tschaikowsky, *Life and Letters of Tschaikowsky,* Lane
D'Indy, *César Franck,* Lane
Gray, *Sibelius,* Oxford Press

CHAPTER XV

Exercise 1. Compare the form and organization of the *Fantastic Symphony* of Berlioz with that of Beethoven's *Fourth Symphony,* listing the differences which you find with regard to type of theme and type of design.

Exercise 2. Examine *Tapiola* by Sibelius. Can you find traces of symphonic organization? What are they? Describe any particularly striking instrumental effects which you find.

Supplementary reading:
Niecks, *Program Music,* Novello
de Pourtales, *Franz Liszt,* Holt
Newman, *Memoirs of Hector Berlioz,* Tudor Press
Newman, *Richard Strauss,* Lane
Rimsky-Korsakoff, *My Musical Life,* Knopf
Lockspeiser, *Debussy,* Dutton
Sabaneyeff, *Modern Russian Composers,* International Publishers

CHAPTER XVI

Exercise 1. Study the development of operatic style from an examination of the following records and note your principal findings.

Peri, *Funeste piaggie* from *Euridice*
Handel, *Lascia ch' io pianga* from *Rinaldo*

Gluck, *Che faro senza Euridice,* from *Orfeo ed Euridice*

Mozart, *La ci darem la mano* from *Don Giovanni*
   Voi che sapete from *The Marriage of Figaro*

Wagner, *Isolda's Liebestod* from *Tristan and Isolda*
   Hagen's Ruf from *The Dusk of the Gods*

Verdi, *Caro Nome* from *Rigoletto*
   Death of Othello from *Othello*

Moussorgsky, *Coronation Scene* from *Boris Godounov*

Debussy, *Je ne pourrais plus sortir duet* from Act 1, *Pelléas and Mélisande*

Exercise 2. Compare the vocal style and musical texture of examples from the choruses of Bach's *Mass in B Minor* and Handel's *Messiah.*

Supplementary reading. General:

Bekker, *The Changing Opera,* Norton (A broad survey)

Kobbe, *The Complete Opera Book,* Putnam (A description of the principal operas)

Dickinson, *Music in the History of the Western Church,* Scribner

Biographical:

Prunieres, *Monteverdi, His Life and Works,* Dutton

Streatfield, *Handel,* Methuen

Schweitzer, *J. S. Bach,* Macmillan

Dent, *Mozart's Operas,* Chatto and Windus

Newman, *Gluck and the Opera,* Dobell

Newman, *Wagner as Man and Artist,* Knopf

Toye, *Giuseppe Verdi,* Knopf

Index

NORTON PAPERBACKS ON MUSIC

WALKER, ALAN, *editor*   The Chopin Companion   N668
WALTER, BRUNO   Of Music and Music-Making   N242
WEISSTEIN, ULRICH, *editor*   The Essence of Opera   N498
WESTRUP, J. A. *and* F. Ll. HARRISON   The New College Encyclopedia
  of Music   N273
WIORA, WALTER   The Four Ages of Music   N427
YOUNG, PERCY   The Choral Tradition   N538